Astra Publications is an imprint of A.
Astra Education Lir.
69, Warren Road
Leyton,
London,
E10 5PZ

First published in Great Britain by Astra Publications 2015

Copyright © Malcolm J Doolin 2015

Malcolm Doolin has asserted his right under the Copyright, Designs and Patent Act 1988 to be identified as the author of this work.

All rights reserved. Apart from any use under UK copyright law no part of this publication may be reproduced, stored in a retrieval system, or transmitted, in any form or by any means, without prior written permission of the publisher, nor be otherwise circulated in any form of binding or cover other than that in which it is published and without a similar condition being imposed on the subsequent publisher.

ISBN 978-0-9935012-0-3

Printed by
Adverset Media Solutions,
Scarborough, North Yorkshire

To the pupils and teachers of Blackhorse Road Boys' School who gave their lives in the Great War, 1914-1919, to John Hemingway who ensured their stories were told and to Eve Wilson who provided the original inspiration, for her enthusiasm and encouragement, and because this was her school.

Malcolm J Doolin
London and Norfolk 2015

The Boys of Blackhorse Road

The Story of an Elementary School War Memorial

by

Malcolm J Doolin

The Boys of Blackhorse Road

The Story of an Elementary School War Memorial

"STEADY"

The Motto of Blackhorse Road Boys' School

"Give All Thou Canst"

The Motto of Willowfield Humanities College

Of the 947,000 allied soldiers who died during the Great War, over 750,000 died at the various Fronts and 128,000 are missing. This is the story of 55 of them.

'As we now are, so once were they; as they now are, so must we be. Let us remember them all, not with bravado or bombast, but with the respect that their sacrifice demands.'[1]

---

[1] Richard Holmes. The Western Front. (BBC Books 1999) p 215

Malcolm Doolin has spent his working life in education, for the last twelve years running his own Consultancy Company, Astra Education Limited. His long time interest in the Great War started when his maternal Grandmother talked of her younger brother, Private Ernest Alfred Sharp, 2nd Battalion The Lancashire Fusiliers, 1898-1918, who, in her words, 'was blown to pieces and has no grave'. Having researched Ernest's life and that of other ordinary soldiers, he completed an M.A. in British First World War Studies with the University of Birmingham where he specialised in the documentary films of Geoffrey Malins and J.B. McDowell who is also connected to Walthamstow but that is another story.

CONTENTS

List of Illustrations   7
Foreword   8

Part 1- The Context in 1914
1. Blackhorse Road School to Willowfield Humanities College   13
2. Walthamstow in 1914   18
3. The International picture in 1914   23
   Map of the Western Front   28

Part 2 - The Boys' Stories
1. 1914 – Frederick Blythe and George Beck   29
2. 1915 – Alfred Johnson, William Johnson, Aubrey Cox, George Atree, Leonard Tebbs, George Bundock, Richard Hooper, Henry Parrott   34
3. 1916 – Frank Hayward, Thomas Chilton, Albert Nankivell, George Stagg, George Shea, Arthur Wood, Arthur Dunford, William Beck, Thomas Green, Percy Spreadborough   45
4. 1917 – Herbert Wills, Francis Mace, Samuel Standcumbe, Thomas Waller, Harry Wilson, Arthur Wiles, James Vickery, Henry Lowings   60
5. 1918 – Ernest Nottage, Frederick Shea, Alfred Smith, Edward Rollings, Archibald Smith, Joseph Pooley, Ernest Harvey, Flemming Goddard, George Allen, Frederick Keen, John Blackmore, William Peachey, Leslie Conway, Reginald Sellers, Jarvis Engley, Albert Smither, Robert Tresadern, Sydney Bartram, Alfred Cox, Sidney Day, Albert Mills, Cecil French, Louis Simmonds, George Mills   81
6. The reports of my death have been greatly exaggerated - Eric Cottew, Stanley Robarts, James Staines   125
7. Conclusion   131
   Acknowledgements   134
   Suggested Reading   136
   Western Front Association; Picture Credits; Bibliography   137

Illustrations

The War Memorial in the old school hall
Map showing the streets around the school in 1913
The Blackhorse Road Schools' site in the early 1960s
The two remaining 'departments', the Boys' School and the Girls' School in 2015
The Boys' School in 2015
One of the school halls from the 1901 building
One of classrooms from the 1901 building
Clifton Avenue houses, opposite the school in 2015
Volunteers waiting to enlist
A British Heavy Gun in Action
A London Heavy Battery in Action
H. M. S. Mantis
A Sergeant in the Seaforth Highlanders
James Vickery's mouth organ and medals
Royal Army Medical Staff in action
Medical Corps bringing back the wounded
Casualties after the battle
The moment before an attack
Troops following up an initial attack
The Silver War Badge
The 'Death Plaque' and scroll and letter from the King
The Menin Gate Memorial
The graves of the four "Boys" buried in Queen's Road Cemetery
Louis Simmonds' grave in the Südfriedhof Cemetery, Cologne
The Thiepval Memorial to the Missing of the Somme

Foreword

Blackhorse Road School, Boys', Girls' and Infants', was built on a site bounded by Tavistock and Clifton Avenues in Walthamstow, North East London, and was the predecessor of Willowfield School, later Willowfield Humanities College. The Infants' Department took boys and girls from 4-7 while from 7-14 they went to the boys' or girls' school. The three separate schools, sometimes referred to as 'departments' of the Blackhorse Road Elementary School,[2] opened on the same site in 1901 to serve the rapidly developing area north of Forest Road.

Because Blackhorse Road was an Elementary School, pupils left at 14. A few won scholarships to go on to a Higher Elementary School[3] but most went into employment and took up work such as clerking, shop work or apprenticeships. Across the country, less than 6% of pupils remained at school after the age of 14.[4]

Over the next 114 years, the school went through changes of name and various rebuilds but much of the original building remains today on the Clifton Avenue site.

For many years, the War Memorial to the Teachers and Old Boys of the Blackhorse Road School, "The Boys of Blackhorse Road", was in the school hall, constructed in the 1960s, before being moved to the entrance hall of the new school on Blackhorse Road. The memorial is copper and was bought by subscription although there is no record now of the manufacturer. It commemorates 55 people, 52 ex-pupils and three teachers, who gave their lives in the Great War 1914-1919. It has been possible to confirm the deaths of 49 of the pupils and all

---

[2] Elementary Schools took pupils from 6 to 14 although the leaving age was 13.

[3] Higher Elementary Schools took pupils from Elementary School who passed a Scholarship examination. Although the places were free, there were costs for parents such as uniform, which meant many pupils from poorer backgrounds could not take up their Scholarship.

[4] Footnote Education: Historical statistics Standard Note: SN/SG/4252 Last updated: 27 November 2012 Author: Paul Bolton Social & General Statistics page 9

three teachers. Of the 52 confirmed deaths, 20 have no known grave and are commemorated on one of the great memorials in France or Belgium. Four came home to die and are buried in Walthamstow Cemetery in Queen's Road. Four pairs of brothers were killed and, in one of these cases, the parents lost their only sons. Four other families lost a second child who did not attend the school. Most of "The Boys" lived at some time in the streets around the school including seven in Blenheim Road. Two "Boys" were killed in the first few months of the war in 1914; seven in 1915 including three as a result of the Gallipoli Campaign; 11 in 1916, all victims of the Somme Offensive; eight were killed in 1917 including four during the Third Battle of Ypres (Passchendaele) and one, the only sailor, in the Middle East. The worst year of the war, however, was 1918 with 24 deaths, most during the Allied Offensive, the 100 days, which forced the German surrender.

We have concluded that three names are on the memorial in error, a not uncommon occurrence with the confusion surrounding war deaths, particularly where there was no body to identify. Of these three, one was still alive in 1972, another lost his brother and was himself severely wounded but not killed whilst the third served and survived but lost a brother with the same initial who did not attend the school. It is also possible that there are names of Blackhorse Road School casualties that are missing from the memorial.

Unlike the Public Schools and Grammar Schools where pupils could remain to 18 or 19 and, in many cases, join the Schools' Officer Training Corps (OTC) which prepared them for officer's commissions when the war came, "The Boys" were all rankers. This is not surprising given their backgrounds. Amongst their number is a Company Quartermaster Sergeant, four sergeants, a corporal, six Lance-Corporals and a further Lance-Corporal who lost his stripe. The only one who had a commission, and then only for a while, is one of "The Boys" who should not be on the memorial.[5] Three won medals for gallantry but not all were well behaved and in some

---
[5] Eric Cottew

instances, committed serious acts of misconduct. What they have in common is that they gave their lives, in most cases their short lives. 27 of "The Boys" were under 21 when they died. The age profile shows the average age at death as 22 years and two months and, when the three teachers are removed, the average is only 20 years and three months.

For Britain the conflict began with the declaration of War on Germany on 3 August 1914. By 20 November 1914, 88 former pupils of Blackhorse Road Boys' School had enlisted. Their names were published by the Headmaster, Mr. R. D. Simpson, as a Roll of Honour in the Walthamstow, Leyton and Chingford Guardian, as was a common practice amongst the local schools.[6] Assuming that they were all at least 16 when they enlisted, they would all have left school by 1911 so they came from the pupils who attended from 1901-1911. About 1,100 boys in total had been on the school roll during those years.

"The Boys of Blackhorse Road" are representative of groups of similar people across the land. Some would have enlisted with their pals, some for the adventure, some for patriotic reasons, some hoping for a better life than the one they were living. It is hard to imagine the impact on the area of the loss of so many, the impact on parents and siblings and, in a few cases, wives and children, particularly as the war went on and most families were affected by loss.

Undertaking any piece of historical research is both stimulating and frustrating. Stimulating because you learn new things, sometimes quite unexpected things; frustrating because the information you seek, however hard you look, is not available. An event as recent in historical terms as the First World War is no exception. Many servicemen's records were destroyed by bombing in September 1940. Those that are left, 'the burnt documents', represent the records of 2.8 of the 7 million men and women who served in the First World War. Many of

---

[6] Walthamstow, Leyton and Chingford Guardian, 20 November 1918, p8

those are partial records. This means that there is only a 40% chance of finding details of a person's military career. Of the 55 names on the Blackhorse Road Memorial, some or all of the military records of 35 have been traced although in many cases little information actually remains. Inevitably, therefore, there will always be gaps in our knowledge of "The Boys". As you will read, for some of "The Boys" we are able to provide a good deal of detail of their lives, for others most of their lives will remain lost, brief lives, barely lived and not remembered.

To research the names on the memorial we sought as much evidence as possible to ensure we had the right people. At least three pieces of evidence were needed before we felt we had identified someone. The School's Registers kept at the archives in Vestry House, Walthamstow, provided On and Off Roll dates, addresses, dates of birth, previous school and father's name. We then linked that information with the Censuses of 1901 and 1911 and, in some cases, 1891 to confirm details and add information on families, occupations and movements. Even then, there is the frustration of incomplete returns, incorrectly written down names, key people being away from home on Census night and possibly being recorded elsewhere but sometimes disappearing completely. At that time, not unlike today, many families moved house and even area quite frequently depending on occupation and financial circumstances. Many lived in crowded conditions with other occupants in what were often two up two down houses. Only 9 (17%) of the 52 pupils were born in Walthamstow. Of the other 43, 18 (35%) came from other parts of East London; 17 (33%) came from parts of North London; 5 (10%) came from South London and 3 (6%) came from outside London. The 'burnt documents' added confirmation, along with information from the Commonwealth War Graves Commission (CWGC) site, the Walthamstow War Memorial site, Regimental Diaries, Regimental Museums, Forces Records, Birth, Deaths, Marriages and Wills records. As a result, we are confident we have the stories of "The Boys" who died and, as has already been explained, evidence that in three cases "Boys" who survived the War and should not be on the memorial.

In researching "The Boys" it became clear that their story was both a study of society at that time and of London and Walthamstow in particular. But their story was also the story of the Great War so that is how we have told it.

Part 1- The Context in 1914

Chapter 1

Blackhorse Road School to Willowfield Humanities College

On 27 February 1899 the Walthamstow School Board agreed to the conveyance of land in Clifton and Tavistock Avenues for the Blackhorse Road Schools.[7] The schools were needed to provide education for the growing population of the area. The population of Walthamstow grew from 46,345 in 1891 to 95,131 in 1901 and the number of houses doubled to 16,000.[8] An article in the local paper of the time reveals that the schools cost £19,983.0.0d[9] with

'a separate block for each of the three departments. The total accommodation is for 1,424, namely 482 boys, 482 girls, and 460 infants. Each block comprises a large central hall with classrooms, etc. Mr. R. D. Simpson, formerly senior master at Coppermill Lane School[10] is headmaster of the boys' school,...'[11]

The article continues stating that

'The schools are excellently designed, and they will be lighted by electricity. They were opened for work on the 27th August, and there were on the register on the 6th inst. 248 boys, 208 girls, and 271 infants.'[12]

Four of the 248 boys are on the War Memorial.

The schools' official opening on Saturday 7 September 1901 was held in the central aisle of the Boys' Department where speeches were made, which have a familiar ring over a century later,

---

[7] Walthamstow School Board Minutes 27 February 1899 p106
[8] A History of the County of Essex, Volume 6. Ed. W. R. Powell (London 1973) pp 275-285
[9] Equivalent to £2,195,890.00 in 2015
[10] Coppermill Road Board School had been open since 1897.
[11] Walthamstow, Leyton and Chingford Guardian 13 September 1901 p3
[12] Ibid

and hymns were sung. In his speech, the Chairman of the Works Committee, Mr R. T. Jolly, referred to the growing school population in Walthamstow which stood at 21,000 and was increasing at a rate

> 'of 1,400 or 1,500 children each year. To keep pace with this increase it was necessary to open a block of schools similar to this one every year.'[13]

He reported that

> 'Considerable opposition was manifested to the purchase of this particular site. Some people said they could get a much cheaper site.'[14]

He concluded his speech by touching on 'the question of secondary education, which was of the greatest importance.'[15] He felt that 'we were, to some extent, behind some countries'. The paper reports that he made a comparison with education in Germany where there lay

> 'our greatest danger, and there the enforcement of secondary education was much more severe than here. The first thing that they learnt in Germany was the English language, because they knew the English were the people they would have to compete with in trade. In this matter of secondary education, parents who wished their children to get on must realise that they must make some sacrifice, for if children were to do any real good they must be kept at school until they were 16 or 17.'[16]

This was met with cheers and he then declared the schools open.

Mr Simpson, in his speech, stressed the importance of parents

> 'sending their children regularly to school, observing that those who sent their children irregularly were unreasonable enough to expect that they would be kept on a level with those who attended irregularly.'[17]

---

[13] Ibid
[14] Ibid
[15] Ibid
[16] Ibid
[17] Ibid

He also 'indignantly denied the suggestion often made that the education in Board Schools was shoddy.'[18]

In the event, the Boys' and Girls' schools were elementary schools and catered for children from 6, when they left the Infants School, to 13 although many at Blackhorse Road stayed until they were 14. Elementary schools had been set up to provide education for the working classes under the 1870 Education Act and were funded from taxes. They were overseen by local school Boards so were often known as Board Schools.

In 1880 school attendance was made compulsory and, in 1891, elementary education was made free. The schools provided a restricted curriculum concentrating almost exclusively on the '3Rs' (reading, writing and 'rithmetic); the teacher's authority was paramount and there was emphasis on punctuality and obedience. Classes were large with a teacher supervising with assistance from a team of older pupils acting as monitors.[19]

By 1900, nearly half of the children who attended public elementary schools were in Board schools: in large urban areas the proportion was often much higher.

It was still very difficult for children to fulfil Mr Jolley's request and stay at school after 13. There were some local Higher Grade school places offering science or Art and, as we will see, some of the Blackhorse Road "Boys" gained scholarships to local ones. Unfortunately, they were not actually free so many parents could not afford to allow their children to go. Also, for some families there was a greater need to having a further wage earner to supplement the family income. The 1902 Education Act created Local Education Authorities and opened the way for more secondary education but it was still not free as there were costs for uniform and some materials. Inevitably, this meant that few working class

---

[18] Ibid
[19] In 1900 there was an average of 42 pupils per teacher (of varying qualification levels). *Education: Historical statistics Standard Note: SN/SG/4252* Last updated 27 November 2012 Author: Paul Bolton Social & General Statistics page 3

children could go on to any form of Higher Education.

Mr Simpson remained at the school until 1 October 1919. He wrote in the School Log that

> 'On August 26 1901 I opened the new school as the Head Master. Today I leave it with much regret. The best years of my life have been given here, filled with much happiness and sacred associations amongst the staff and lads. I have been promoted to the Headship of the North Central School[20] where I take up my duties on November 3rd. R. D. Simpson'[21]

He had seen the school through its first 18 years, had seen many of his 'lads' go off to war and would have known the ones who failed to return. He attended the funeral of at least one of "The Boys".

Strangely he does not refer to the unveiling of the School War Memorial and we learn of that only from the Girls' School Log Book.[22]

> 'The girls of the school visited the Boys' Dept. this morning to see the War Memorial towards which they had contributed. They were away about 10 minutes.'

This places the unveiling in September 1920 but, unfortunately, we can not trace any other records about it.

There is not time here to do justice to the full history of the school and all the changes it underwent. It took in older pupils; had pupils evacuated during the Second World War and had unexploded bombs drop in its playground. In 1945 it was re-organised for juniors and infants and in 1963 for infants only. Blackhorse Road School for Girls became mixed in 1961; new buildings were completed in 1962 and it was re-named as Willowfield. In 1968 Willowfield Secondary School became an 11-14 Junior High School, for many years under the leadership of the much loved Mr and Mrs Foster.

---

[20] North Central School – probably Greenleaf Road Higher Elementary School.
[21] Blackhorse Road Boys' School Log Book 31 October 1919
[22] Blackhorse Road Girls' School Log Book 19 September 1920

In September 1986 it became Willowfield Comprehensive School under Alan Steel, taking pupils from 11-16. From September 1996 until April 2011, Eve Wilson was Headteacher, followed by the current Headteacher, John Hemingway who had been a teacher and Deputy Head at the school since 1986. On 26 June 2009, to reflect its specialism, the school became Willowfield Humanities College and, in September 2015, it moved into its new premises adjacent to Blackhorse Road Station.

Chapter 2

Walthamstow in 1914

At the turn of the 20th Century Walthamstow was a rapidly developing area. The Blackhorse Road Schools were opened in 1901 and between 1894 and 1913 the area was developed from fields to high density housing. The Ordnance Survey Map of Walthamstow (West) for 1894[23] shows a few houses on the west side of Blackhorse Lane north of Forest Road with The Royal Standard Public House standing where it does today. Blackhorse Road Station, opened in 1894, was then on the opposite side of Blackhorse Road.[24] There was no housing on the north side of Forest Road between Blackhorse Lane and Higham Hill Road and little on the south side. South and east of Stoneydown there was denser housing. Plots of land became available for development around the turn of the century and by 1913[25] housing had developed along both sides of Blackhorse Lane as far as Blenheim Road and on both sides of Forest Road between Blackhorse Lane and Luton Road. The unbuilt land opposite the station had also been in-filled leaving only the goods yard. The school was surrounded by new housing including Clifton, Pembar and Tavistock Avenues, although the east end of Clifton Avenue and the Forest Road land behind it remained unbuilt on. The houses were two storey terraced dwellings often divided into flats or multi-occupied. Most of the building south of Forest Road was carried out by the Warner Estate Company. By 1914, West Walthamstow had become the most densely populated part of Walthamstow. North along Blackhorse Lane were numerous factories providing employment for both men and women, whilst

---

[23] Old Ordnance Survey Maps. Walthamstow (West) 1894. The Godfrey Edition 2010
[24] The station was rebuilt across the road when the Victoria Line Station was built in 1968 and the old station was demolished in 1981.
[25] Old Ordnance Survey Maps. Walthamstow West 1913. The Godfrey Edition 2010

the local station provided transport to the docks and the stations in north and west London. To get to the City, commuters would have used either St James' or Hoe Street[26] Stations. Cheap workman's tickets were available on early trains to get people to work.

Many of "The Boys" and their fathers and mothers would have worked locally. The housing boom created employment for some, whilst for others the demands of the growing population generated work in shops and factories. The Blackhorse Lane area saw considerable industrial development and employment with a printing and engineering company, Peter Hooker Limited, opening their premises in Blackhorse Lane in 1901. During the Great War they produced aircraft engines. In 1902, The Micanite and Insulators Company moved to Blackhorse Lane from Stanstead Mountfitchet and during the First War employed over 600 staff. The Fuller-Wenstrom Electrical Manufacturing Company who built motors moved into Blackhorse Lane in 1905 and later into Fulbourne Road. Fulbourne Road also housed the premises of Hawker Siddeley. Buses were built in Blackhorse Lane from early in the century. From 1909, The London General Omnibus Company began producing motor omnibuses in premises inherited from Vanguard at Blackhorse Lane. In 1912, they were bought out by The Associated Equipment Company (AEC), a branch of The Underground Group. During the war the factory produced buses to be used as troop carriers, as well as building military trucks.

Walthamstow in the pre-war years was well served with entertainment with cinemas, music halls and many pubs including the Walthamstow Palace Theatre[27] on Walthamstow High Street, which opened on the 28 December 1903 and seated over 1,600 people. During the war, Music Hall was one of the main forms of entertainment and often provided patriotic propaganda to aid recruitment. At that time, the Palace presented Music Hall but often

---

[26] Hoe Street Station – now Walthamstow Central.
[27] The Walthamstow Palace Theatre closed in 1954 and was demolished in 1960.

included short films in its programmes. Walthamstow had many cinemas including the Victoria Picture Palace which, as the King's Theatre,[28] had become Walthamstow's first cinema in 1906.[29]

The film historian Kevin Brownlow says that 'The motion picture came of age during World War I.'[30] Local audiences would have laughed at Charlie Chaplin films such as *The Tramp* ' and epics such as *The Birth of A Nation* ' and *Intolerance* 'and also seen films made in the local Walthamstow Studios. One of the local film makers, J. B. McDowell,[31] was to play a significant part in recording the war.

Audiences would not have seen much about the war in their visits to the cinema. The government and the military had stopped any filming of the war and censored reporting. However, in late 1915, the government recognised that, with so many people visiting the cinema, films would make excellent propaganda that would be seen by the mass of the population. They commissioned Geoffrey Malins[32] and McDowell to make battlefield films. The most famous of these was *The Battle of the Somme*', which filmed the build up and first day of the battle. Described as 'the most important propaganda film produced by any of World War I's combatants',[33] it was shown across the country, in Europe, America and the Empire and to troops behind the lines, although reports indicate they would rather have seen a Chaplin film. There can be little doubt it would

[28] The EMD (Granada) Cinemas now stands on the site.
[29] In Walthamstow and Leyton people had the choice of at least six other cinemas.The Queen's, Hoe Street; The Empire at Bell Corner; The Scala at the Baker's Arms; The King's Hall in Leyton; the St James's in St James's Street and the Princes in the High Street.
[30] K.Brownlow, *The War, the West and the Wilderness* (London: Secker and Warburg, 1979), p. 3
[31] J. B. (John) McDowell (1878-1954) was Director of the British and Colonial Film Company, based in Walthamstow.
[32] Geoffrey Malins, (1886-1940) worked on several feature films before becoming a freelance war correspondent in Belgium and France filming newsreels.
[33] D. Culbert, *The Imperial War Museum: World War I film catalogue and 'The Battle of the Somme'* (video). (London, Historical Journal of Film, Radio and Television, Volume 15, No. 4, 1995), p. 575

have been seen by many of "The Boys". It would also have been seen by their families, when it was screened in Walthamstow, so they would have gained an idea of what their sons were involved in. It is also possible that the film was edited at McDowell's studio in Walthamstow.

Walthamstow was well served with other entertainment such as pubs, concerts, lectures and dances. The Public Baths in the High Street provided a full programme during the winter months whilst, in 1915, an Antiquarian Society was established there. Next door to the Baths was the Central Library, opened in 1909. For those wanting a day in the fresh air, Lloyd Park had been opened in 1900.

As now, what Walthamstow did not have was a professional football team. Association football was growing in popularity in the early years of the 20th Century and it became increasingly common for working men to hold back their admission fee from their wages. In those pre-Wembley days, the 1913-14 F.A. Cup Final was played at the Crystal Palace between Burnley and Liverpool in front of nearly 73,000 spectators with Burnley winning 1-0. As now, for Walthamstow residents to watch football, they had to travel out of the area. Tottenham Hotspur were established at White Hart Lane although the 1913-14 season saw them finish seventeenth out of twenty teams in the First Division. In 1913, Arsenal dropped the pre-fix Woolwich when they moved from south-east London to Highbury. They were playing in the Second Division and finished third with 49 points from 28 games, six points above Clapton Orient who were sixth. Clapton Orient moved to Leyton in 1937. The other local club, West Ham United were playing in the Southern League. Football in the borough was represented by Walthamstow Avenue, an amateur team playing at Green Pond Road,[34] off Higham Hill Road. They played in the Walthamstow and District League.[35]

---

[34] Green Pond Road off Higham Hill Road. Housing stands on the site.
[35] Founded in 1900, they closed in 1988 when they merged with other local clubs to eventually become Dagenham and Redbridge.

Despite the many changes in Walthamstow over the past 100 years, it is a sobering thought that if any of "The Boys" or their parents were to return to their old school today they would recognise much of the area. While much of the external fabric of the school remains, as do many of the houses they lived in, they would doubtless find the volume and speed of traffic startling and their quiet streets and avenues are no more. The house may have undergone modernisation with changed frontages, new roofs, plastic or metal windows and doors, rear and front extension and lofts but most retain the basic design and many of the houses they lived in are still standing. They would have been amazed by the new school building, standing where the railway goods yard was situated, but walking the streets around both of the schools they would doubtless have seen much that was familiar.

Chapter 3

The International picture in 1914

During the early years of the 20th Century the major powers of Europe formed alliances aimed at strengthening their positions and maintaining a balance of power that prevented any one country from dominating the continent. Great Britain, with a huge empire which covered much of the globe, was allied from 1903 with her traditional enemy, France, through the Entente Cordiale. In 1907 Britain allied with Russia to form the Entente Alliance. Geographically located between France and Russia was the alliance of Germany, a new country formed in 1879, and the declining Austro-Hungarian Empire. As well as Austria and Hungary, the Austro-Hungarian Empire included most of the modern Balkan states, many of which were keen to become independent. On 28 June 1914 the heir to the Austro-Hungarian throne, Archduke Franz Ferdinand and his wife, Sophie, were assassinated on an official visit to Sarajevo, Bosnia, by Bosnian Serbs keen to gain Bosnian independence. The Austro-Hungarian Empire imposed 10 demands on the Serbs, all of which were met. Russia supported Serbia in her desire for independence and mobilised her army whilst Austro-Hungary looked to Germany for support. On 31 July 1914, the German Kaiser issued an ultimatum to Russia to cease mobilisation. The following day at 7.30 p.m., with no reply received, Germany declared war on Russia. On 2 August Germany invaded Russia's ally, France, at several points including through Belgium using the Schlieffen Plan which aimed at a swift invasion though northern France, brushing the North Sea and encircling Paris and forcing the French to surrender. Germany demanded unhindered passage for her troops through Belgium. However Belgium, formed in 1839, was protected by the Treaty of London, signed in 1839 by France, Great Britain and Germany. Britain honoured the Treaty and issued Germany with an ultimatum to withdraw her troops from Belgium by midnight on 4 August. The ultimatum expired and Britain declared war on Germany.

The third power to join the Central Powers of Germany and Austro-Hungary was the Ottoman Empire (Turkey). With the signing of the Turco-German Alliance on 2 August 1914 they formed the Triple Alliance. Turkey formally entered World War I on 28 October 1914 with the bombing of Russian Black Sea ports and the Allied Powers declared war on the Ottoman Empire on November 4.

It is likely that Germany underestimated Britain. However Germany had been building her navy and army and looking to develop her own Empire and that provided a potential threat to the British Empire. Whilst the majority of the British population may have been unaware of the prospect of war, writers and politicians had recognised this threat for some time with books including 'The Riddle of the Sands' by Erskine Chiders, 'Spies of the Kaiser' and 'The Invasion of 1910' by William Le Queux and plays such 'An Englishman's Home' by Guy Du Maurier all portrayed the growing threat Germany was starting to pose with stories of invasion from Germany.

For British politicians at the time there was much more concern over growing industrial unrest, and demands for Home Rule for Ireland and votes for women than over activities in Europe. Only 50% of men had the vote and no women. Britain's overseas interest was her empire. Some 435 million people, a quarter of the world's population, owed allegiance to Britain. In addition to raw materials and food, it provided much of the wealth for the middle and upper classes. In 1914, despite the country's wealth, 1% of the population controlled 70% of the wealth and the average wage for a man for a 58 hour week varied from 16 shillings (80p) to £1.14s. 4d. (£1.71p)[36] Of the 5 million women employed half were paid from 10s. (50p) to 15s. (75p) per week, or less than half a man's wages. The average life expectancy for men was 50 years, for women 54. The disparity

---

[36] In 1914, £1.0.0. was the equivalent of approximately £103.00 in 2015. Wartime inflation caused prices of many goods to double by 1918 but in 1914, the average price for a pint of beer was 1d; a pint of milk cost 1d; 12 eggs 8d. http://www.thisismoney.co.uk/

between living in east and west London was over 20 years in favour of the west. To seek a better life, one in twenty people emigrated to Australia, Canada and the USA. After 1908 there was increasing industrial unrest and strikes as workers argued for better rewards. Much of the wage went on accommodation and food and the army offered regular wages and food. It also required a strong navy to keep the shipping lanes open for trade and to deal with any local issues that may occur. The converse was a very small peace time regular army of 247,500 of which about half was based overseas to protect the Empire, supplemented by the Reservists, mainly ex-soldiers, and Territorials,[37] who spent part of their annual holidays training, and by the Indian Army. Unlike Germany, Russia and France, there was no regular military service so when the war came, Britain had by far the smallest army to deploy. Germany could call upon over 4,000,000 men, Austro-Hungary nearly 2,000,000, Turkey 210,000, France nearly 4,000,000 and Russia nearly 6,000,000.

At midnight on Sunday 4 August 1914 the British ultimatum to Germany expired. The news was met with cheering from crowds who gathered outside public buildings across the land. In Walthamstow the local paper reported 'Stirring scenes have been witnessed in our town this week...' as 'Men, women and children gathered in thousands to watch' the local Territorial Army the 7th Battalion of the Essex Regiment, entrain from Hoe Street Station[38] for the 'seaside town' of Felixstowe which they had been ordered to defend. Across London the scenes were repeated as men rushed to enlist, encouraged by the newspapers.

---

[37] The Territorial Force was created in 1908 and was originally intended to provide a home defence force of part-time soldiers. Men were not obliged to serve overseas until 1916 and the troops undertook to serve full-time in the event of general mobilisation.

[38] Walthamstow, Leyton and Chingford Guardian 5 August 1914 p5

On 5 August 1914, Field-Marshal Lord Kitchener[39] became Secretary of State for War. He was one of the few senior figures to predict a long and costly war and to foresee that the existing British Expeditionary Force (BEF) of six infantry divisions and four cavalry brigades would be far too small to win the war. He decided to raise a series of volunteer 'New Armies', each duplicating the original BEF. His first appeal was issued on 7 August. 478,893 men joined the army between 4 August and 12 September, including 33,204 on 3 September alone. They became known as 'Kitchener's Army'. (See Illustrations section)

We know that "The Boys of Blackhorse Road" played their part in the recruitment drive as the local paper published lists of the various school's ex-pupils who had enlisted. By 20 November 88 ex-pupils of Blackhorse Road School had volunteered.[40] Fourteen of these would not survive the war.

There are various reasons why men enlisted. For some it was patriotism and the call to the colours. For many it was the sense of adventure, perhaps taking them from the humdrum existence of their daily lives. Most ordinary people had hardly travelled beyond their local area so joining the army provided a chance to travel. For others it was the chance of a better life with regular food and wages.

For some it was the collective will, generated from such as workplaces and sports teams with friends and workmates joining up, fighting and, in many cases, dying together; for others it may have been the pressure to go and 'do your bit'. We may assume that at least some of "The Boys" enlisted together. As the war progressed and moved in to 1915 and beyond, the flow of volunteers slowed. Schemes, such as Lord Derby's,[41] were introduced to increase

[39] Field-Marshal Lord Kitchener of Khartoum, 1850-1916. Secretary of State for War 1914-1916.
[40] Walthamstow, Leyton and Chingford Guardian 20 November 1914 p8
[41] Lord Derby's scheme aimed to increase recruitment and avoid conscription by allowing men to attest for service at a later date. Men who attested would be paid one days wages, placed in the army reserve and allowed to continue their civilian life until needed by the military. They wore a khaki armband.

recruitment culminating in conscription. As we will learn, this was to be the way with "The Boys".

It is unlikely that many of the recruits envisaged either the dangers they were to face or the length of the war. There was a popular view that 'the war would be over by Christmas' although Kitchener predicted it would last until at least 1917. His theory was based partly on the time it would take to prepare and equip an army capable of defeating Germany and partly on the way the war was likely to be fought. The war would not be won by winning a series of battles as in previous campaigns but of a more remorseless wearing down of the enemy interspersed with major attacks. He was to be proved right except that the war continued into late 1918.

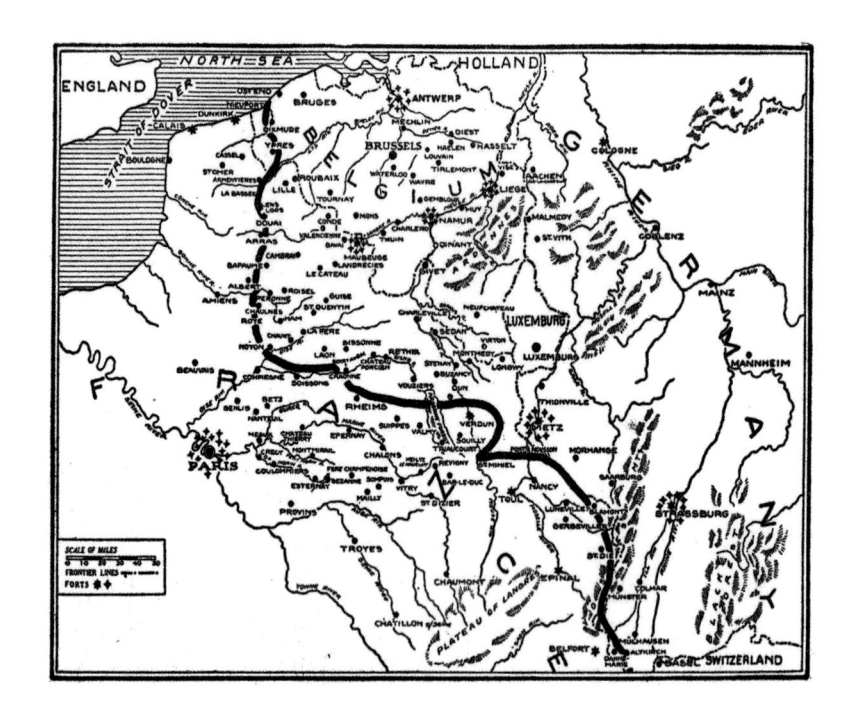

The Western Front

Part 2 - The Boys' Stories

Chapter 1

1914

Frederick Blythe and George Beck

Following Germany's declaration of war on France on 2 August, the German invasion achieved initial success. The Belgian government evacuated on 17 August and Brussels was captured on 20 August. By the end of the month, the university town of Louvain had been sacked and its magnificent library destroyed. Reports of other atrocities, were circulating. By 18 August the British Expeditionary Force (BEF) had been mustered and sent to France to support the French, the first time a British Force had entered France to help her. The British and German armies met at the Battle of Mons on 23 August and the BEF was forced to retreat towards the River Marne. With Russia on the offensive in the east, Germany had to send troops to fight there, weakening her western army. Germany defeated Russia at the Battles of Tannenberg (26-30 August) and the Masurian Lakes (9-14 September).

In early September 1914 the German advance on Paris was halted at the Battle of the Marne and the Germans retreated to high ground north of the River Aisne. Amongst the BEF was **Frederick (Fred) Henry Blythe**. Born in Mile End on 31 December 1891, his parents, Daniel, a corn porter, and Annie had two older children and the family lived at 101, Oxford Street[42], Stepney. Frederick was baptised on 13 January 1892 at St Philip's Church[43], Stepney. Between 1892 and 1894 the family moved to Walthamstow and in 1901[44] the family were living at 28, Gloucester Road, off Blackhorse

---
[42] Oxford Street, now known as Stepney Way.
[43] St Philip's Church, 1838-1979
[44] 1901 Census carried out on 31 March 1901.

Lane, and there were now five children. Frederick joined Blackhorse Road School from Gamuel Road School[45] as one of the first intake of pupils on 27 August 1901. His journey to Gamuel Road involved a round trip of nearly four miles every day, which it is likely he would have had to walk, so moving to his new local school would have cut his daily journey by about three miles. However, Frederick remained at the school for only two and a half months before the family left the area.

Frederick was 18 and working as a barman when he enlisted as a regular soldier on 11 May 1909 for a six year term, to be followed by six years in the reserves. By April 1911[46] the family were living in Bow and Daniel was working as a Car Man, a driver of a horse drawn vehicle. By then, Frederick had 11 brothers and sisters of whom 10 survived.

Frederick was a Gunner Layer[47] in 29th Battery,[48] 42nd Brigade[49] of The Royal Field Artillery. He would have been working with horses and may have gained experience with horses from his father, the Car Man. The RFA formed part of the BEF 3rd Division,[50] one of the first formations to go to France. They took part in most of the early engagements of the war including the Battle of the Aisne between 12-15 September 1914. Frederick became the first "Boy" to die, aged 22, when he was killed in action in the Brenelle Valley of the Aisne on 13 September 1914. He was also the first to have no known grave and is commemorated on the La Ferte-Sous-Jouarre

---

[45] Gamuel Road Board School opened in 1883 for girls and infants, and for boys from 1887.
[46] 1911 Census carried out on 2 April 1911.
[47] The Gunner Layer trained the gun on its target.
[48] A Battery was a group of guns.
[49] A Brigade was a unit of between three and six battalions, each battalion comprising between 300 and 800 men.
[50] A Division comprised several regiments or Brigades totalling between 10 and 20,000 soldiers.

memorial.[51] Details of his death were scarce and both his father and Mary Bishop (possibly his girlfriend) of Rotherhithe wrote to the War Office seeking information.

The BEF managed to halt the German advance to the North Sea east of the Belgian City of Ypres. For the rest of the War Ypres was under constant German attack from three sides as the Allies defended the Salient.[52] By the end of the War the city was all but flattened and over 1,700,000 lives had been lost in the town and surrounding area. Had it fallen, the Germans would have had their breakthrough to the Channel and been able to launch bigger naval attacks on the British supply lines from the Empire and the USA. It became crucial for the Allies to hold the town against all odds and Ypres took on a symbolic status. Ypres was the scene of major battles in 1914, 1915, 1917 and 1918 as the allies attempted counter-attacks. Nine of "The Boys" died in the area and five of them have no known grave.

The first of these to die was **George Beck**. George Charles Beck was born in Haggerston on 1 January 1895 and was the younger brother of William who was to die at the Somme in 1916. In 1901, the family were living at 17, Trafalgar Road, Haggerston, with parents William, an engine fitter and turner, and Mary Ann, three siblings and three lodgers, George, Emma and Henry Lewis. The family moved to Walthamstow in 1901 or 1902 and George attended Blackhorse Road Infants' School, transferring to the Boys' School on 2 June 1906. He left shortly before he was 14 on 18 December 1908. The family lived initially at 77, St Andrew's Road, Walthamstow, north of the school and by 1911 were a few roads south to 53, Bunyan Road. His father was working on a bread, biscuit and sweet machine and George, aged 16, was a greengrocer's assistant. There were now eight children.

---

[51] La Ferté-sous-Jouarre memorial or The Memorial to the Missing of the Marne commemorates over 3,700 BEF with no known grave, killed in the area in August, September and early October 1914.

[52] Salient – a piece of land or section of fortification jutting out into enemy territory.

Given that George died in November 1914, he too must have been serving in the regular army. The new volunteers were not trained and sent to fight until the spring of 1915 at the earliest. His name appears, along with his brother's, in the newspaper article of 20 November 1914 naming the ex-pupils who had enlisted.[53] Sadly, George was already dead. He had enlisted in Stratford and served as a Private in the 1st Battalion, The King's (Liverpool) Regiment. The regiment was part of 2nd Division and was sent to France on 13 August as one of the original components of the BEF. They were one of the first Divisions involved in action on the Western Front and remained there throughout the war. They saw action at Mons, the Aisne and the First Battle of Ypres. George died on 11 November 1914, aged 19, of wounds suffered in fighting in the region of Hoord, West Hock. He has no known grave and is commemorated on the Menin Gate Memorial[54] at Ypres. His father duly received his outstanding pay of £7.4s.0d (£7.20p)[55] on 24 April 1915 followed by a further sum of £0.2s.9d (14p) on 29 July 1915 and his War Gratuity of £5.0s.0d on 30 June 1919.[56] He was posthumously awarded the British War and Victory Medals.

---

[53] Walthamstow, Leyton and Chingford Guardian 20 November 1914 p8
[54] The Menin Gate. Designed by Sir Henry Blomfield and unveiled by Lord Plumer on 24 July 1927, it is the main western entrance to Ypres and was placed there as thousands of troops left by that route to fight in the salient. (See Illustrations section).
[55] All soldiers were paid until their death so outstanding pay would be the amount owed on his death.
[56] The war gratuity was introduced in December 1918 as a payment to be made to men who had served for a period of 6 months or more home service or for any length of service overseas.

By the end of 1914, the war had reached Britain as Scarborough, Whitby and Hartlepool were shelled by German naval vessels and nearly 50 people were killed. The armies were digging in with the trench lines[57] reaching from the North Sea to the Swiss border. The war was not going to be over by Christmas.

---

[57] Trenches – the nature of the trenches depended on the terrain and how easy it was to dig down. German trenches tended to be stronger, often reinforced with concrete. The trenches were usually in three lines; the front line trenches; a support trench, usually with dug outs for shelter, and a reserve trench. The trenches were not dug in straight lines but in sections to prevent damage from shell blasts affecting the whole line. The distance between the trenches was known as 'no man's land' and varied from 30 yards to several hundred yards.

Chapter 2

1915

Alfred Johnson, William Johnson, Aubrey Cox, George Atree, Leonard Tebbs, George Bundock, Richard Hooper, Henry Parrott

The first two "Boys" to die in 1915 were brothers, Alfred and William Johnson.

Alfred Richard Johnson was born in Bow on 25 January 1893. In 1901 he was living with his parents, Alfred and Kate and four siblings, Ernest, Arthur, Elsie and William, at 54, Fairfield Road, Higham Hill, Walthamstow. His father was a stenotype printer. Alfred and William joined Blackhorse Road School together on 20 April 1903 from Gainsford Road School,[58] by which time they had moved a few roads north to 27, Cumberland Road in Higham Hill. Alfred left school on 13 February 1907 in his fourteenth year. In 1911 Alfred, William, one sister and their parents were living at 6, Shaftesbury Road, further south in the borough, and Alfred was working as a printer's reader. Based on when he was killed, he must have already been in the army. Like his brother, he is named in the newspaper article listing those who had joined up.[59] He served in the Scots Guards as a Gunner, possibly infilling for the casualties the regiment had suffered as part of the BEF in 1914.

On 10 March 1915 the Allies attempted to break through the German line at Neuve Chapelle. At this time most of the Allied trenches were held by the French as the new British army was being trained. The battle was intended to break the German lines, and allow an advance to Aubers Ridge and possibly as far as Lille. The

---

[58] Gainsford Road Board School opened in 1902 and renamed William Morris in 1903 because it was built on land adjoining Elm House, where he lived. It went through various changes before closing in 1932.

[59] Walthamstow, Leyton and Chingford Guardian 20 November 1914 p8

battle had limited success. 300 yards were gained and the village of Neuve Chapelle was taken but at a cost of 12,000 casualties, one of whom was Alfred. He was wounded and taken to No. 7 Casualty Clearing Station,[60] Merville, where he died on 28 March, aged 22. He is buried in Merville Communal Cemetery, about 15 kilometres north of Bethune and about 20 kilometres south-west of Armentieres. There is a mystery surrounding his War Pay as on 27 November 1915 £4.10.11d (£4.55p) was paid to Rachel E Precious and on 9 July 1919 a further sum, this time of £3.0.0d was paid to Rachel E. Precious, his sole legatee. We may assume this was a girlfriend although, according to the records, his next of kin were his parents.

Less than two months later, Alfred's younger brother, **William Henry Johnson**, was killed. He was born on 16 January 1895 in Bow and joined the school from Gainsford Road School with his brother on 20 April 1903. He left school on 23 December 1908 shortly before his fourteenth birthday. Unlike his brother, William's occupation is not given on the 1911 Census. William was serving as a Private in the 1st Battalion, The Somerset Light Infantry when he was killed on 25 May 1915, aged 20, during the Second Battle of Ypres.[61] The Somerset Light Infantry were stationed at Colchester in August 1914 as part of the 11th Brigade of the 4th Division. They were sent to France on 22 August and fought at Le Cateau, the Marne, the Aisne and Messines prior to

the Second Battle of Ypres. It is likely that William was also a regular soldier although it is possible he was a volunteer, infilled into the regiment to replace casualties. His death date places him

---

[60] Casualty Clearing Stations (CCSs) were part of the casualty evacuation chain. They treated men so that they could return to duty or be evacuated to a Base Hospital. Most were on or near railway lines. CCS locations can often be identified from the cemeteries that surrounded them.

[61] The Second Battle of Ypres consisted of six engagements, Gravenstafe, 22–23 April; St. Julien, 24 April–4 May; Frezenberg, 8–13 May; Bellewaarde, 24–25 May; Hooge, 30–31 July and the Second Attack on Bellewaarde, 25 September.

at Bellewaarde however the confusion of battle and the lack of accurate records means this cannot be certain. He has no known grave and is commemorated on the Menin Gate Memorial.

Neuve Chapelle and Second Ypres showed up a severe shortage of shells, vital equipment if the enemy lines were to be 'softened up' by a heavy bombardment prior to the troops attacking. As a result, David Lloyd George, M.P.,[62] the Chancellor of the Exchequer, was moved to a new post as Minister of Munitions to increase the number of shells being produced. He ensured that many factories ceased their peacetime production and produced war weapons instead. These included some of the factories on Blackhorse Lane. The increased demand created the need for additional labour and, with many men enlisting, their places were taken by women, albeit they were paid at a lower rate.

Aubrey Victor Cox also died as a result of injuries sustained in the Second Battle of Ypres. He was invalided home and is buried in Queen's Road Cemetery, Walthamstow. Born in Peckham on 12 October 1897 he was, at 17 and a half, the second youngest "Boy" to die in the War. The family moved to Walthamstow soon after his birth as he was baptised in Walthamstow on 5 December 1897. By 1901 they were living at 21, Maude Terrace, just off Blackhorse Road, Walthamstow. His father, John H, was a butcher, and he and his wife, Maude Adelaide, had one other child, Eva, who was then one year old. Maude's brother, Henry Cox, was also living in the house. Henry John (or John Henry) died on 31 August 1903 leaving £145.12s.0d (£145.60p) to his widow, which would be worth about £16,000 today. By then the family were living at 19, Essex Grove, now demolished, which was off Forest Road, close to Blackhorse Road Station. Aubrey joined Blackhorse Road School from the Infants' School on 3 April 1904. The family had moved again, to 30, Blackhorse Lane. Aubrey left the school on 22 December 1905 when he moved

---

[62] David Lloyd George, 1863-1945. Chancellor of the Exchequer 1908-1915; Minister of Munitions 1915-1916; Prime Minister 1916-1922,

to St Saviour's School.[63] St Saviour's School was attached to the church of the same name and it seems highly likely that the change of school was related to Aubrey attending a church school. This is supported by a document of his which is lodged at the Imperial War Museum (IWM). It is a tract from the Religious Tract Society, number 499, called 'For the Last Time', which presumably was in his possession when he died. Also, at his funeral, vicars from two churches presided.

Aubrey changed schools again as, on 13 September 1910, aged almost 13, he must have obtained a scholarship as he joined Hackney Downs School,[64][65] where he remained for two years, then going on to Sir George Monoux School.[66][67]

The family was living at 30 Blackhorse Lane in 1911 and Aubrey now had three siblings Eva, 11, Rita 9 and Daphne 7.

Aubrey was working for a city electrical engineering firm, Verity and Co. of 31, King Street, Covent Garden when he enlisted, along with several other employees, in the autumn of 1914.

The IWM also has four postcards Aubrey sent to his cousins Jack and Bob Fuller, whilst training at Aldershot in 1914.[68] Two are photographs of groups of soldiers which presumably include Aubrey although neither card has names. One was posted to Master Jack Fuller, 68, Beaulah Road, Hoe Street, Walthamstow, the other was unposted. The other two are silk postcards, one saying 'Forget Me Not' and the other 'Remember'. On the back of the 'Remember' card in Aubrey's handwriting is the word 'Jack'.

---

[63] St Saviour's School off Markhouse Road was linked to St Saviour's Church on Markhouse Road.
[64] Hackney Downs, formerly the Grocers' Company's School. Founded 1876. Grammar School 1906-1969. Closed 1995. Re-built and re-opened in 2004 as Mossbourne Academy.
[65] Hackney Downs School Roll of Honour http://www.cloveclub.com/wp-content/uploads/WW1ROHa.pdf
[66] Sir George Monoux Grammar School then situated in the High Street had a small number of free places but most pupils were fee paying.
[67] Walthamstow, Leyton and Chingford Guardian 11 June 1915 p5
[68] IWM record K11/1191 and K11/1192

On 29 September 1914, Maude Adelaide died, aged 41, and was buried with her husband in Queens Road Cemetery, Walthamstow.

Having completed his training Aubrey was posted as a Rifleman to the 12th Battalion, the County (City) of London Regiment (The Rangers). The Regiment had been stationed in Bedford Square at the outbreak of War and were moved to the Sussex Coast before being deployed to guard the Waterloo railway line. Sent to France in December 1914, they were initially used to defend communication lines before seeing action at the Second Battle of Ypres.

Aubrey was severely wounded by shrapnel during the battle on 9 May and was invalided back to England. He died of septicaemia from his wounds in Abbots Barton Voluntary Aid Detachment (VAD) Hospital[69] near Canterbury on 1 June 1915.

The IWM has a typed report of his death which states that the first part of his funeral was held in Canterbury on 3 June 1915 with a bearer party from the 6th Dragoon Guards. The regimental band played the 'Dead March from Saul' as the cortege went to Canterbury East station. Aubrey had a polished oak coffin with brass fittings, draped with a Union Jack, carried on a Royal Field Artillery gun carriage. Mistakenly, the report states that his final internment was at Barry Avenue, Stamford Hill on Saturday.

The Walthamstow, Leyton and Chingford Guardian reported his funeral on Monday 7 June, 'The Last Post; Young Hero Buried in Walthamstow Cemetery'[70] and the Blackhorse Road Boys' School Log Book carries an entry stating that the Headmaster, Mr Simpson 'attended the funeral of Rifleman Aubrey Cox.'[71] The Headteacher of St. Saviour's Boys' School, John Cox, stated that his school was represented by pupils and that 'eight of my old boys have been killed in action out of the 174 who

---

[69] Abbots Barton was owned by Francis Bennet-Goldney, 1865-1918. Mayor of Canterbury 1905-1910 and M.P. 1910-1918, he gave the house to the military as a hospital. It is now a hotel.
[70] Walthamstow, Leyton and Chingford Guadian 11 June 1915 p5
[71] Blackhorse Road Boy's School Log Book 7 June 1915

are with the forces.'[72] Aubrey was posthumously awarded the British War Medal and Victory Medal and the 1914-1915 Star. He is buried with his parents in Queen's Road Cemetery, Walthamstow, the first of four "Boys" to be buried there. Aubrey does not have a Commonwealth War Graves headstone and is instead commemorated on the family headstone. Sadly, the headstone to the three of them is now leaning heavily to the side. (See Illustrations section)

On 21 December 1915, his outstanding pay of £4.19.4d (£4.97p) was sent to his Grandmother, Mary A Rough and on 8 July 1919 she received his War Gratuity of £3.0.0d.

With no advance on the Western Front, a plan was devised to attack Germany's ally, the Ottoman Empire (Turkey), and attempt to link with Russia, thus, providing a stronger threat to Germany's eastern border. The plan was spearheaded by the first Lord of the Admiralty, Winston Churchill,[73] despite strong opposition from the First Sea Lord, Admiral Fisher.[74] The Gallipoli, or the Dardanelles, Campaign was also an attempt to control the sea route from Europe to Russia. In the build up to the attack, troops were sent to Egypt for training and acclimatisation. The naval attack on the Dardanelles began with a long-range bombardment by British and French battleships on the Dardanelles Straits on 19 February 1915 which failed. The Turkish forces abandoned their outer forts but met the approaching Allied minesweepers with heavy fire, stalling the advance. On 18 March 18, allied battleships entered the straits. Turkish fire from the shore and undetected mines sank three of the ships and severely damaged three others. The major

land invasion of the Gallipoli Peninsula by British and French troops, as well as divisions of the Australian and New Zealand Army Corps (ANZAC), began on 25 April.

Gallipoli saw some of the fiercest fighting of the war but a

---
[72] Walthamstow, Leyton and Chingford Guadian 11 June 1915 p5
[73] Winston Churchill, 1875-1965. First Lord of the Admiralty 1911-1915.
[74] Admiral John (Jackie) Fisher, 1841-1920. First Sea Lord 1904-1910; 1914-1915.

lack of sufficient intelligence and knowledge of the terrain, along with fierce Turkish resistance, impeded its success. By mid-October, Allied forces had suffered heavy casualties and had made little headway from their initial landing sites. A combination of intense heat, swarms of flies, body lice, severe lack of water and insufficient supplies combined to make it one of the worst places to serve. Evacuation from Gallipoli began in December 1915, and was completed early the following January at a cost of 213,000 casualties of which 145,000 were from illness.

Three of "The Boys" were to die as a result of the campaign, two in hospital in Malta and one at Gallipoli. **George Daniel Attree** was born on 28 June 1894 in Islington, the third of six children, one of whom was deceased. His parents were David, a Police Constable, and Mary. In 1901 the family were living at 4, Hervey Park Road, Walthamstow, south of Forest Road. George joined Blackhorse Road School when the school opened on 27 August 1901 from Coppermill Road School[75] and left on 14 November 1908 aged 14. At the time of the 1911 Census the family were still living in Walthamstow having moved about half a mile east to 500, Forest Road and George was working as an assistant salesman in the boot trade.

George enlisted at Leyton in August 1914 and served as a Private in the 1st/7th Battalion, The Essex Regiment, along with George Bundock.

At the outbreak of war, the 1/7th was stationed at Walthamstow, as part of the Essex Brigade of the East Anglian Division. With the 1/6th they were moved to Norwich and, in April 1915, they became the 161st Brigade of the 54th Division. On 21 July 1915, the Brigade embarked from Plymouth to Lemnos en route to Suvla Bay where they landed on 12 August. Within a fortnight, George was killed on 25 August and is buried in Azmak Cemetery, Suvla Bay, Gallipoli. He was 21. On 16 June 1919, his mother received

---
[75] Coppermill Road Board School was opened in 1897.

£2.2s.6d (£2.12.5p) as his War Gratuity.

George Henry Bundock, sometimes known as Henry Bundock, was born on 13 March 1898 in Shoreditch. In 1901 the family were living at 105, Chewton Road, Walthamstow, a turning off Blackhorse Road. His father, Henry, was a labourer and his mother was called Emma. He had two older brothers and a younger sister. George joined Blackhorse Road School on 3 April 1904 from the Infants' school. By then, the family, like the Attree's, were living in Hervey Park Road, a little further north off Forest Road, in their case at number 25. By 1911 there was another daughter and they had moved two houses to 29, Hervey Park Road. George left school, aged 14, on 22 March 1912. He enlisted before November 1914[76] and served as a Private in the 1st/7th Battalion, The Essex Regiment, along with George Attree. He was wounded at Suvla Bay and taken to hospital on Malta where he died on 12 December 1915, aged 17, the youngest "Boy" to die in action. He is buried in Pieta Military Cemetery, the main garrison cemetery on Malta. His death was reported in the local paper on 8 October.[77]

On 4 December 1915 the regiment was evacuated from Gallipoli to Mudros owing to severe casualties from combat, disease and harsh weather.

The third "Boy" to die as a result of Gallipoli was **Richard James Hooper.** Born in Highbury on Christmas Eve 1896, in 1901 the family were living at 35, Calabria Road, Islington. His father, also Richard James, was a linotype operator and he and Florence had three other children, two girls and a boy. He joined Blackhorse Road from the Infants' on 11 April 1904 by which time the family were living at 13, Tavistock Avenue. On 31 January 1908 he was taken off roll to be admitted to hospital and was re-admitted to the school on 27 April. The Off Roll Register reports that he was taken off roll again on 26 June 1908 when he

---

[76] Walthamstow, Leyton and Chingford Guardian 20 November 1914 p8
[77] Walthamstow, Leyton and Chingford Guardian 8 October 1915 p5

left the district. However, on 4 November 1910, according to the School Log Book, he won a Scholarship to the School of Art.[78] In 1911 his father was described as a compositor and another sister had been born but one other child did not survive. Richard's older brother, Sidney, was working as a cinematograph operator in the developing cinema industry. His father, Richard, died on 11 January 1913 and his mother re-married in 1915 to Thomas Glazer.

Richard enlisted at Handel Street, London,[79] before November 1914 and served as a Private in the 1st Battalion London Regiment (Royal Fusiliers).[80] We do not know his occupation but the fact that he enlisted in Bloomsbury, rather than locally, indicates he may have been working in London. The regiment was formed in London in September 1914 and moved to Kent to join the 2/1st London Brigade of the 2/1st London Division. In February 1915 it was deployed to Malta and on 27 August to Alexandria. On 25 September 1915 it landed at Suvla Bay attached to the 88th Brigade of the 29th Division and engaged in various actions against the Turkish Army.

Richard Hooper was wounded on Gallipoli and evacuated to hospital on Malta where he died aged 19, on 5 November. He too was buried in Pieta Military Cemetery.

In January 1916, the regiment was evacuated from Gallipoli to Egypt owing to severe casualties from combat, disease and harsh weather. In April the regiment landed in Marseilles and was moved to Rouen. In June 1916 it was disbanded.

On 4 October 1917, Richard's elder brother, Sydney the cinematograph operator, now serving as a Private with the 1st Battalion East Surrey Regiment was reported missing in one of the battles, probably Broodseinde, that formed part of the Battle of Passchendaele (Third Ypres). He was officially declared dead on 10 October and his remains are buried in Hooge Crater Cemetery just

---

[78] School Log Book 4 November 1910
[79] Handel Street is in Bloomsbury and there is still an Army Recruiting Office there today.
[80] Walthamstow, Leyton and Chingford Guardian 20 November 1914 p8

east of Ypres.

Whilst the Gallipoli campaign was being waged through 1915, the war on the Western Front continued and two further "Boys" lost their lives.

Leonard Tebbs was born in Brighton on 21 December 1895. In 1901 the family were still living in Brighton where his father, Frederick, was working as a brush maker's finisher. He and his wife, Louisa, had nine children of whom Leonard was the eighth. Within a year there was a further brother and all 10 were still alive in 1911. Leonard was admitted to Blackhorse Road School on 14 September 1903 from Eldon Road School, Edmonton,[81] along with his older brother William. The family were living at 47, Clarence Road, north of the school off Blackhorse Lane. Leonard left school on 21 December 1909 on his fourteenth birthday. By 1911 the family had moved to 70, Mount Pleasant Road in Higham Hill. Frederick was still working as a brush maker's finisher and Leonard was employed as a cycle repairer. By 1915, they had moved again, to 25, Markhouse Road, Walthamstow, near the junction with Markhouse Avenue.

Leonard enlisted soon after war was declared.[82] He served as a Private in the 10th Battalion, The Essex Regiment. The 10th Battalion was formed at Warley in September 1914 and was then moved to Shorncliffe Camp, Folkestone, as part of the 53rd Brigade of the 18th Division before being moved to Colchester. In March 1915 the regiment was moved to Codford St. Mary. On 26 July 1915 they were mobilised for war and landed at Boulogne. They were operating in the Somme region near Albert when Leonard was killed by a mine on 28 August. He was the 10th Battalion Essex Regiment's first casualty of the war and was 19 years old. The local paper reported his death, noting that he was an 'active member of the Walthamstow Branch of the Sons of Temperance and was very

---
[81] Eldon Road Board School opened 1899. There is still a school on the site.
[82] Walthamstow, Leyton and Chingford Guardian 20 November 1914 p8

popular with members.'[83] On 27 December 1915, a sum of £6.0.0. outstanding pay was paid to his father. A further sum of £2.14.10 (£2.74p) was paid on 27 December and his War Gratuity of £3.0.0. was paid on 30 August 1919. He is buried in Norfolk Cemetery, Becordel-Becourt, 2.5 Kilometres east of Albert.

The last "Boy" to die in 1915 was **Henry Parrott** who was killed when his trench, known as Forward Cottage, north of Ypres, was shelled on 17 December 1915. He has no grave and is commemorated on the Menin Gate. Henry George Parrott was born in Walthamstow on 12 November 1895 and in 1901 was living at 46, Markhouse Road. His father, Robert, was a carpenter and he and his wife, Mary Ann, had six children, five boys and a girl. Henry joined Blackhorse Road from Gamuel Road School on 31 August 1908. By then the family had moved to 56, Blackhorse Road. On 26 November 1909, according to the School Log Book, he won a Scholarship to the School of Art and was described as the 'Top boy in Walthamstow'. He left school on 26 November 1909 aged 14. In 1911[84] he was working as an office boy at a watch and clock importers so presumably he did not, or could not, take up the scholarship. His father was working as a journeyman carpenter engaged in house building and the family had nine children of whom two were deceased by 1911, thus, it is highly unlikely the family could afford the additional costs of Henry's higher education. Henry enlisted soon after war was declared.[85] He gained rapid promotion and at the time of his death was serving as a Sergeant in 'D' Company, the 8th Battalion, The Bedfordshire Regiment. On 28 April 1916, his father was paid Henry's outstanding pay of £2.16.3 (£2.83p) and his War Gratuity of £8.0.0 was paid on 7 September 1919.

---

[83] Walthamstow, Leyton and Chingford Guardian 10 September 1915 p23
[84] 1911 Census
[85] Walthamstow, Leyton and Chingford Guardian 20 November 1914 p8

Chapter 3

1916

Frank Hayward, Thomas Chilton, Albert Nankivell, George Stagg, George Shea, Arthur Wood, Arthur Dunford, William Beck, Thomas Green, Percy Spreadborough

1916 was a year of campaigns on many fronts. By 9 January 1916 the last allied troops had been evacuated from Gallipoli. The final toll is approximate but Allied losses totalled over 60,000 killed, including 50,000 British Empire and French and 10,000 ANZAC, and 242,000 wounded and missing. Ottoman losses totalled over 57,000 killed and 110,000 wounded and missing.

The main focus of the War reverted to the Western Front where, on 21 February 1916, the Germans launched an attack on the French in the area of Verdun in Eastern France. Fighting continued for over nine months until 18 December when the Germans finally withdrew. The details of the action do not fit into this story but its importance to the French was high and its impact on the war significant. To fight the Germans at Verdun the French needed to move troops from the northern front line causing the British to lengthen their defence lines. The French also put pressure on the British to launch an attack in northern France to distract the Germans from Verdun. The Allied Commander in Chief, Sir Douglas Haig[86] believed that the decisive battle to win the war would be fought in the Ypres area but had to succumb to political pressure to fight in the Somme region.

---

[86] Field Marshal Douglas Haig, 1st Earl Haig, (1861–1928) commander of the BEF from 1915-1918.

The British planned to attack on a 24 kilometre (15 mile) front between Serre, north of the Ancre, and Curlu, north of the Somme and the French divisions would attack on a 13km (eight mile) front south of the Somme, between Curlu and Peronne. Prior to the attack, allied artillery bombarded the German lines for a week, firing 1.6 million shells. The intention was to smash the barbed wire in front of the trenches and weaken the German defences. The bombardment gave the Germans warning of an impending attack and they moved in to their well constructed bunkers under their heavily fortified trenches and waited for the bombardment to cease. The sound of the guns was so loud they were heard in London. In fact, the shelling failed to destroy the barbed wire and when the firing ceased the Germans left their bunkers and set up their positions to repel the attack.

From 7.20 a.m. on 1 July, a series of mines were exploded under the German lines and at around 7.30 a.m. whistles blew to signal the start of the attack. The British troops had been ordered to walk towards the German trenches and expect little resistance. Once they had been seized, cavalry units would pour through to pursue the fleeing Germans. As the British divisions walked towards the German lines, the machine guns started. A few units managed to reach the German trenches but they could not exploit their gains and were driven back. By the end of the day, the British had sustained 57,470 casualties, including 19,240 killed, the heaviest ever losses in a 24 hour period suffered by the British Army. Sixty per cent of all officers involved on the first day were killed.

Many of the troops were part of the new volunteer army including groups of men from the same town or works or clubs who enlisted together to serve together in local regiments such as the Accrington 'Pals', the Grimsby 'Chums' and the Hull 'Commercials'. The problem was that in fighting together, many such units had heavy casualties. For weeks local newspapers carried lists of dead, wounded and missing. The French were more successful but were also unable to exploit their gains and had to retreat to earlier positions.

The objective became more limited and the British concentrated on the southern sector of the line. They took the German positions on 14 July but could not follow through and the advance became a stalemate, with little ground gained. Various attacks were carried out over the ensuing months and these were later named as battles, usually of the village or strongpoint under attack. On 15 September the offensive was renewed, using tanks for the first time but they made little impact. In October torrential rains turned the battlegrounds into a quagmire and on 18 November the battle ended, with the Allies having advanced only 8km (five miles). The British suffered approximately 420,000 casualties, including the loss of 10 of "The Boys of Blackhorse Road". The French lost 195,000 men and the Germans 650,000. However high the losses, nevertheless it is worth remembering that it was fought primarily to support the French at Verdun where defeat could have seen them out of the war. In that respect it may be seen as successful.

The first "Boy" to die on the Somme was **Frank Hayward** who was killed in action on 5 July. He was 19 years old and a Gunner in 'A' Battery, the 154th Brigade of The Royal Field Artillery. The Brigade fought as part of 36th (Ulster) Division from early 1915 and at the Somme they attacked a major German stronghold, the Schwaben Redoubt, north of Thiepval Woods. On the 1st July they lost 5,104 casualties with approximately 2,069 dead.

Frank Richard William Hayward was born on 7 August 1896 in Walthamstow and was baptised on 27 September 1896. In 1901 the family were living at 172, Forest Road, close to the school. Frank's father, Edwin, was a builders' foreman and he and Mary Ann had five other children. In 1901, the oldest married daughter and her son were living with the family. One of Frank's older brothers was Bertie, then aged 8. The family had moved to Walthamstow in the late 1880s, possibly because of the building work in the area. Frank joined Blackhorse Road School from the Infants' on 11 April 1904 and left on 11 March 1911, aged 14. By then the family were living at 11, Stoneydown Avenue, Walthamstow, and Frank went to work as an assistant in a woollens shop. There had been 11 children of whom three had not survived. Frank enlisted in 1915 as one of 'Kitchener's Army'. He is buried in Knightsbridge Cemetery, Mesnil-Martinsart. His body would have been brought there from a battlefield cemetery after the Armistice.

Less than a year later, on 28 May 1917 Frank's older brother was serving as Private Bertie Hayward with the 2nd/10th London Brigade near Arras when he was killed in action. He has no known grave and is commemorated on the Arras Memorial.[87]

Of the 10 "Boys" to die at the Somme, eight have no known grave and are commemorated on the Thiepval Memorial.[88]

Albert Edward Nankivell was born on 28 February 1890 in Stoke Newington. In 1891[89] his family were living at 19, Brodia Road, Stoke Newington. His parents were William, a house carpenter, and Martha and he had three older siblings. Two other people lived in the house, a not unusual occurrence at the time. By 1901 the family were living at 45, Higham Hill Road, Walthamstow, and there were a further two children. Albert joined the school on 2 September 1901 from Higham Hill School[90] and left on 26 February 1904, shortly before his fourteenth birthday. By 1911, aged 21, he

---

[87] The Arras Memorial is in the Faubourg-d'Amiens Cemetery in Arras. It commemorates nearly 35,000 men from the United Kingdom, South Africa and New Zealand who died in the area between spring 1916 and August 1918 and who have no known grave.

[88] The Thiepval Memorial to the Missing of the Somme bears the names of over 76,000 men of the United Kingdom and South Africa who were killed in the Somme area before 20 March 1918 and who have no known grave. Designed by Sir Edwin Lutyens and built between 1928 and 1932, it was unveiled on 1 August 1932. Eight of "The Boys" are commemorated here, the most in any one place. (See Illustrations section)

[89] The 1891 Census was carried out on 5 April 1891.

[90] Higham Hill School, St. Andrew's Road, existed before 1870. It was taken over by the School Board in 1880 and a new school, the first to be built by the Board, was opened for 1,102 children in 1883 and enlarged in 1902.

was working as a clerk and living with his parents and five siblings at 18, Albert Road, off Hoe Street, Walthamstow. The family had six children living and one was deceased.

Albert enlisted in 1914 and served as a Private in the 9th Battalion, The Essex Regiment. He arrived in France on 27 July 1915. The regiment fought at Loos in September 1915. In July 1916 the regiment fought at the Somme and Albert was killed on 10 August, probably at Pozieres, aged 26. His name is one of 949 officers and men of the Essex Regiment on the Thiepval Memorial. On 9 February 1917 his mother as his sole legatee was paid his outstanding pay of £2.18.4d (£2.92) and on 24 September 1919 his War Gratuity of £9.0.0d. He was awarded the 1914-1915 Star, the British War Medal and Victory Star in 1919. His military record shows his name sometimes spelt as Nankwell or Nankwill, doubtless an error in transcription.

Thomas William Chilton was born on February 2 1897 in Kings Cross. In 1901 he was living in tenement 14 'B', Block B, Beaconsfield Buildings,[91] Islington, with his parents George and Sarah Jane, and four siblings. His father was a blacksmith. He joined Blackhorse Road School on September 9 1904 from Gifford Street School,[92] Islington and left on 24 February 1911, aged 14. In 1911 the family were living at 9, Farnborough Avenue, Walthamstow, two streets from the school. There were eight children of whom six had survived.

Thomas was working as a grocer's assistant when he enlisted in Stratford on 1 September 1914 and is one of "The Boys" named in the local newspaper.[93] He was 5 feet 5 ½ inches tall with a fresh complexion, brown hair and brown eyes. He was deemed 'fit to serve' and on 4 September he was posted to the 7th Battalion, The Rifle Brigade (The Prince Consort's Own) along with other 'Kitchener volunteers'. Before he had left England, however, he was

---

[91] Beaconsfield Buiildings consisted of 478 tenements in 15 Blocks and was on the site of Bingfield Park and 8 Rufford Street.
[92] Opened 1872 as Gifford Street Board School. Now closed.
[93] Walthamstow, Leyton and Chingford Guardian 20 November 1914 p8

in trouble. On 13 September he was absent from tattoo until 8.50 p.m.[94] and confined to barracks for two days. From 29 October–5 November he was hospitalised in Aldershot with tonsillitis. He was again absent from tattoo from 5-7 March 1915 whilst on active service and guilty of insubordinate conduct. He was confined to barracks for three days and was stopped eight days pay, about 9 shillings and four pence (£0.47p).

The regiment was sent to France on 20 May 1915 and saw service in the Ypres Salient including the German gas attack at Hooge. Thomas was serving on the Somme as a Rifleman when he was killed in action, aged 19, on 18 August 1916, probably in the Delville Wood battle. According to his brother, his mother having died, aged 54, on 13 March 1916, his personal effects were to be sent to his father, who was living at 12, Ritchings Avenue, just across Forest Road from Farnborough Avenue. They were finally sent to his father at 55, Cornwallis Avenue, (probably Road) on the Warner Estate off Blackhorse Road, on 1 October 1919. We can only speculate why George Chilton moved so frequently. Thomas's death was reported in the local paper on 29 September 1916.[95]

George Thomas Stagg was born in Stratford on 30 January 1895. In 1901 the family were living at 32, Napier Road, West Ham, with his father, Thomas, a plumber, his mother Rosina, and one younger sibling, William. George joined Blackhorse Road School on 27 November 1905 from Farmer Road School,[96] Leyton, with his brother. They were now living at 12, Reness Road, Walthamstow, a few roads east of the school. George left school, aged 14, on 5 March 1909 and by 1911 was working as an apprentice printer. The

---

[94] Tattoo – time specified to be back in barracks.
[95] Walthamstow, Leyton and Chingford Guardian 29 September 1916 p6
[96] Farmer Road School, now George Mitchell School. Opened 1903. Jack Cornwell, who was to win a posthumous V.C. at the Battle of Jutland in 1916, joined Farmer Road School, aged five, in May 1905 but it seems unlikely, given the age difference, that their paths would have crossed.

family had moved around the corner to 48, Pasquier Road and there was a younger sibling.

George enlisted at Saint Paul's and served in the 1st Battalion, the Queen's (Royal West Surrey Regiment). By August 1916 he was a Lance Corporal but on 24 August he was killed in action in the High Wood attack. He was 20 years old. His death was reported in the local paper on 29 September.[97] On 28 February 1917 his father was paid his outstanding wages of £0.2.7. (13p) and on 23 September 1919, he was paid George's War Gratuity of £7.0.0d.

George Shea and his older brother Frederick both served and died in the war. George was born on March 15 1897 in Manor Park. In 1901 he and Frederick were living with their maternal Grandmother, Amelia Coutirier,[98] at 209, Clapham Road where she is described as a bookseller. The bookshop was in Holywell Street. (See Frederick Shea) George joined Blackhorse Road School from the Infants' on 3 April 1904. He was then living at 8, Nicholson Road, Walthamstow,[99] with his father, also called George. Enrolling the brothers at Blackhorse Road in 1902 and 1905 are the only references we can find to George senior. He is absent from the Census returns and is dead by 1911 thus, given the seven children he and Frances had, it is possible he followed an itinerant profession or was in the Army or Navy.

By 1911 George was living further east at 425, Forest Road with his mother, Frances, a widow of independent means, and two of his four siblings. A further three children had died. He left school on June 7 1912 aged 15; it is a mystery as to why he was still at the school after 14.

George enlisted in Hornsey in March 1916 when he was 18. He was serving as a Rifleman in the 1st/5th Battalion, The London Regiment, when he was killed in action at the Battle of Guillemont

---

[97] Walthamstow, Leyton and Chingford Guardian 29 September 1916 p6
[98] On the 1891 Census Amelia is noted as a hairdresser living at 299, Strand.
[99] Nicholson Road was a cul-de-sac off Forest Road near Blackhorse Road. It was demolished in the late 1960s and replaced with flats.

on the 6 September 1916 in the attack at Louze Wood, aged 19.

Louze Wood, known to the troops as 'Lousy Wood', was seen as an important objective in the attack on Guillemont as it provided protection to the approaches of Combles, Guillemont and Ginchy. When Haig visited the area on 4 September he made it clear that the capture of the wood and nearby high ground was of the utmost urgency. The southern end of the wood commanded the low ground between Hardecourt and Guillemont. Although not as badly damaged as Delville Wood or High Wood its undergrowth was filled with German barbed wire and defensive posts. The fighting was intense and confused and it was some days before George's death was confirmed. His body was not recovered.

Three of the names on the school memorial are those of teachers who taught at the school between 1901 and 1914. Two of those died at the Somme and are commemorated on the Thiepval Memorial.

Arthur Isaac Wood, at 30 years old, was the second oldest "Boy" to lose his life. He was born in Tottenham on 20 October 1885. In 1891 he was living at 26, Castlewood Road, Hackney with his parents, Stephen, a fancy leather goods maker, and Elizabeth, and four older siblings. By 1901 he was 15 and employed as a Pupil School Teacher[100] and was living at 75, Lennox Road, Walthamstow, with his parents and siblings. On 2 September 1901 he began work at Blackhorse Road Boys' School having been passed to become a Pupil Teacher on 22 July 1901.[101] He left on 31 March 1905[102] 'having completed his apprenticeship'.[103] In 1911 he was living at 224, St John's Road, Walthamstow, and working as an Assistant School Master. His parents and three of his siblings were at the same address. There had been nine children of whom four were deceased.

---

[100] Pupil School Teachers started at 15 and had to study, as well as teach, as part of their training to become teachers. Arthur Wood completed his training in 1905, aged 19. Class sizes were often large.
[101] School Log Book 22 July 1901
[102] 31 March was, at that time, the end of the Educational School Year.
[103] School Log Book 31 March 1905

He enlisted at Leyton in April 1916 and was posted as a Private to the 15th formerly the 1st/13th Battalion, of the London Regiment (The Kensington Battalion) who were serving in the Somme area.

The village of Ginchy, a German strongpoint, had been under attack since 3 September and was now a mass of shell holes and shattered masonry. Its capture was vital to continue the allied line and avoid leaving any Germans behind the advance. On 9 September the village was attacked, supported by the 56th Division including Arthur's regiment, attacking in nearby Leuze and Bouleaux Woods. The village was rushed and taken with heavy casualties and, despite German counter attacks, was held. Arthur was killed on 9 September and his body was never identified. The local paper reported him as the 'first Walthamstow teacher to lay down his life for his country'; he had been 'a scholar at St Mary's School,[104] a pupil teacher at Blackhorse Road and, for the last nine years, a teacher at Higham Hill School[105] and the William Elliott Whittingham School.'[106] It added that this year his 'widowed mother and three sisters,'...'have also lost Mr Wood's father and brother.'[107] Arthur's father had died aged 77 and his brother, Ernest, aged 40. At the time of his death, Arthur was living at 18, Carnarvon Road, Leyton. On 19 October 1916, probate on his estate of £533.1.10d (£533. 9p), a very significant sum for 1916, was granted to his mother. On 2 January 1917 his mother, as his sole executor, was paid his outstanding pay of £2.5.5d (£2. 27 1/2p) and on 15 August 1918 his War Gratuity of £3.0.0d, although there is no evidence it was claimed.

Arthur Dunford taught at Blackhorse Road for three years as a Pupil Teacher. He was born in Shadwell on 14 December 1889. In 1891 he was living with his parents, Thomas, a Police Constable, his mother Annie and eight older siblings at 1, Alms

---
[104] Probably St. Mary's school, Church End.
[105] Higham Hill School, St Andrew's Road. Opened 1883. Demolished and rebuilt as Edward Redhead School. Later Hillyfields School.
[106] William Elliott Whittingham Boys' Council School, Higham Hill Road, opened in 1911 and closed in 1959.
[107] Walthamstow, Leyton and Chingford Guardian 20 October 1916 p3

Houses, Glamis Road, Shadwell.[108] By 1901 they were living at 61, Gosport Road, beside Walthamstow Cemetery, with his parents and five older siblings, the oldest of whom was 28, and his nephew, George. His father was retired by then. According to the School Log Book Arthur commenced duties as a Pupil Teacher on 25 July 1905 after three years at the Walthamstow Technical Institute.[109][110] He left on 31 July 1908 having 'finished his apprenticeship and discontinued his duties at the school'.[111] In 1911 he was working as a school teacher with Walthamstow Urban District Council and still living at 61, Gosport Road. His parents were still alive and two of his siblings and his nephew still resided there. Arthur was working at the school in January 1914 as the Log Book records that he was given 'the power to administer corporal punishment under the committee rules'[112] so presumably he had qualified as a teacher and was now permitted to punish boys by caning them.

He enlisted on 6 April 1916 and served as a Private in the 1st/15th (County of London) Battalion, (The Princess of Wales' Own Civil Service Rifles). The regiment was serving in the Somme Region and, from 15-22 September, took part in the Battle of Flers-Courcelette, an attempt to break through the German lines. The battle saw tanks used for the first time. Arthur's regiment, part of the 47th (1/2nd London) Division, succeeded in clearing the last German-held sections of High Wood, but suffered heavy losses in the process, one of whom was Arthur who was reported wounded and missing on 22 September. He was 26 and his body was never recovered. Arthur's death was reported in the local paper on 10 November

---

[108] Glamis Road is a turning off The Highway leading to Wapping Wall where The Prospect of Whitby Public House is located.
[109] Technical Institutes were funded by grants from the rates and provided laboratory equipment and evening science schools. Two of the largest were Walthamstow, (Grosvenor House), opened in 1897, and Leyton (at the side of the Town Hall), opened in 1898.
[110] School Log Book 25 July 1905
[111] School Log Book 31 July 1908
[112] School Log Book 30 January 1914

1916.[113]

A year later, on 30 October 1917, his 39 year old elder brother John, husband of Lizzie, of 3, Berwick Road, Walthamstow and also of the London Regiment was killed in action during the Third Battle of Ypres. Like Arthur, he has no grave. He is commemorated on the Tyne Cot Memorial.[114]

On 22 November 1917 a photo of Arthur was unveiled at the school.[115] Sadly, no record of this remains.

The next ex-pupil to die, **William Beck,** the younger brother of George who had died on 11 November 1914 near Ypres, was born in Haggerston on 11 February 1893. In 1901 he was living at 17, Trafalgar Road, Haggerston. His father, William, was an engine fitter and turner and he and his wife, Mary, had three other children. Three other people were also living in the house. By 21 January 1902 when he joined Blackhorse Road School from Queen's Road School[116] they were living at 77, St Andrew's Road, Walthamstow, north of the school off Blackhorse Lane. He left on 5 February 1907, shortly before his fourteenth birthday. In 1911 he was working as a metal polisher and living at 53, Bunyan Road, a few roads from the school. His father was described as an engineer's turner on a bread, biscuit and sweet machine and there were now seven younger siblings.

William enlisted in Shoreditch at the start of the war and is named in the newspaper article.[117] He achieved promotion to Lance-Corporal in the 8th Battalion, The Norfolk Regiment. The regiment served on the Western Front from July 1915 and fought at the Somme in 1916.

[113] Walthamstow, Leyton and Chingford Guardian 10 November 1916 p6
[114] The Tyne Cot Memorial to the Missing forms the north-eastern wall of Tyne Cot Cemetery, 9 kilometres from Ypres (Ieper). It commemorates almost 35,000 officers and men whose graves are not known and who died after 16 August 1917.
[115] School Log Book 22 November 1917
[116] Queens Road Board School opened in 1900 with accommodation for 1,434 pupils.
[117] Walthamstow, Leyton and Chingford Guardian 20 November 1914 p8

The Battle of the Ancre Heights from 1 October–11 November 1916, was the continuation of British attacks aimed at securing high ground which would deprive the Germans of observation towards Albert to the south-west and give the British observation north over the Ancre valley to the German positions around Beaumont Hamel, Serre and Beaucourt. Many smaller attacks had been made despite the bad weather which had turned the ground and roads into rivers of mud. William was reported killed in action, amongst heavy casualties, on 21 October, probably in the region of the Schwaben Redoubt near Thiepval. He was 23 years old. On 12 February 1917, £7.4.6d (£7.22 1/2p) outstanding pay was paid to his father with a further sum for his War Gratuity of £9.0.0d on 7 October 1919. He was awarded the 1915 Star whilst still a private on 25 July 1915 and later the family were sent his British and Victory Medals. Neither William nor George has a grave.

William Beck is now commemorated on the Thiepval Memorial. His name is a recent addition to the Addendum Panel. When we began this research his name was commemorated only on The France (1914-1918) Memorial.[118] The change is because the Commonwealth War Graves Commission, having carefully examined his case, have concluded that there is sufficient evidence for his name to be added to the memorial. His omission may be because of his being missing in action and his name was not formally recorded in the correct location where he is believed to have been killed.

Thomas John Green attended Blackhorse Road School from 29 February 1902 until 16 March 1906. He was born in Bethnal Green on 16 March 1892. He was baptised on 3 April in St James the Great Church,[119] Bethnal Green. The family were living at 34, Charlotte Street, (also known as Turin

---

[118] The France (1914-1918) Memorial is the database kept at the Commonwealth War Graves Commission Headquarters in Maidenhead, Berkshire and commemorates casualties who died in France for whom no grave could be found.

[119] St. James the Great Church, Bethnal-Green Road. Built 1840-44. Deconsecrated in 1984 and converted to residential use.

Street) Bethnal Green. His father, also Thomas John, was a card box cutter. Three children, probably of the mother, Jane's first marriage, and a son of the current marriage resided in the house but on Census Day, Thomas was absent. He was an institutional patient at Oxford House, 59, Station Road, Bexhill-On-Sea. There were five other patients, all from London. From 1911-1974 there are records of children being sent there from the Queen Elizabeth Hospital in Hackney so it is probable that he was convalescing from an illness.[120] In 1902 the family moved to Walthamstow and lived at 48, Melbourne Road, off Palmerston Road, south of Forest Road. Thomas had been attending Turin Street Board School[121] in Bethnal Green. He left school on his fourteenth birthday and by 1911 was working as a wine merchant's clerk. The family were now living at 42, Ickworth Park Road, further west and nearer the school, with one sibling and mother's daughter and her husband. One child had died.

Thomas enlisted in Walthamstow in May 1916 and served in the 11th The Royal Sussex Regiment. By October 1916 he had been promoted to Lance-Corporal. The Royal Sussex Regiment were serving at the Somme and took part in a series of attacks to clear the Schwaben Redoubt. It fell on 14 October but further operations were delayed because of the weather and the terrible battlefield conditions. Renewed attacks were made on 21 October to take Regina trench and Stuff trench. After sharp fighting all of the objectives were taken in just over 30 minutes and the whole of the crest of the ridge was now in British hands. Thomas was killed on the same day as William Beck, 21 October. He was 24. His grave is in Mill Road Cemetery, where his body would have been brought from a battlefield cemetery after the Armistice.

Percy William Spreadborough has the distinction of living nearest to the school at 27, Clifton Avenue when he died and of being the last "Boy" to die as part of the Somme Campaign. Percy

[120] http://www.nationalarchives.gov.uk/hospitalrecords/details.asp?id=2100&page=33
[121] Turin Street Board School, 1875-1929. The building still exists.

was born on 25 January 1894 at 31, Kings Square, off the Goswell Road, Islington. His mother, Amelia May, died when he was two and in 1901 he and his father, Ernest, a carpenter and joiner, were living at 25, Clifton Avenue with his step-mother, Jane, and his sister. There is no record of Ernest and Jane marrying (or of Jane at all after 1901), however, on 26 December 1901, Ernest, a widower aged 35, married Celia Porter Hook, a spinster aged 35, at St Simon's Church, Chelsea.[122] Both gave their address as 183, Pavilion Road, Chelsea.[123] Ernest's profession is noted as carpenter but nothing is recorded for Celia. Celia's father was a mariner. Ernest's was a Sanitary Inspector.

On 12 June 1902 Percy joined Blackhorse Road School from the Infants' School. On 9 June 1905 he left the district but was re-admitted on 24 July 1905, finally leaving on 9 November 1908 aged 14. By 1911, the family had moved to 27, Clifton Avenue and Ernest was working as a carpenter and joiner with a firm of undertakers. The family house also accommodated two boarders. At that time, Percy was working as an office boy with a book seller but by 1 July 1915, when he enlisted in Stratford, he was working as a fitter's mate.

His military record was not without incident. He was serving as a Rifleman in the 17th Battalion, The King's Royal Rifle Corps when on 1 March 1916 he was confined to barracks for two days for refusing to give his name to an NCO.[124] The regiment was sent to France on 8 March and served in the Somme area. On 6 June 1916 Percy suffered a self-inflicted wound to his forehead when another soldier's rifle caught in his kit as Percy was attempting to shoot down a pigeon coming from the German lines. Although it

---

[122] St Simon's Church, near Cadogan Square, Chelsea. Opened 1859.
[123] It was not uncommon for both parties to give the same address when one lived outside the parish to ensure they qualified by residence to be married in the local church.
[124] NCO – Non-Commissioned Officer was an officer who has achieved promotion without a commission, e.g. Lance-Corporal, Corporal, Sergeant, Sergeant Major, Warrant Officer.

was reported, no further action was taken. He was killed in action on the 22 October, aged 22, in the same conflict as William Beck and Thomas Green and close to where Thomas Green died. His body was never recovered and he is commemorated on the Thiepval Memorial.

On 28 March 1917 a payment was made to Charlotte Camber, his sole legatee. A letter from the War Office to Records on 27 April 1917 states that any medals should be sent to Miss Charlotte Ellen Camber of 6, Diana Road, Walthamstow. On 22 October 1919 a further sum of £5.0.0d was paid to Charlotte Camber/Cambwer as his sole legatee and, on 22 October 1919, his personal effects were sent to her. All soldiers had to make a will in case they were killed and we may assume that, in naming her as his legatee, she was in a relationship with Percy.

In 1911, a Charlotte Ellen Camber, born 1891, was working as a kitchen maid at 65, Wimpole Street, London, in the household of Thomas Henry, Lord Sanderson, a peer of the realm. In early 1919, she married Alexander Dinmock in West Ham, which would explain why, despite the War Office letter of 22 October 1919 and Charlotte being his sole legatee, on 5 May 1920 Percy's step-mother, Celia Porter Spreadborough, was sent his death plaque and scroll. She also received his British War and Victory Medals on 25 May 1921.

After two years of war, on 4 December, Prime Minister Herbert Asquith resigned and was replaced on 7 December by Lloyd George. A War Cabinet was instituted, replacing the War Committee.

Chapter 4

1917

Herbert Wills, Francis Mace, Samuel Standcumbe, Thomas Waller, Harry Wilson, Arthur Wiles, James Vickery, Henry Lowings

1917 was to prove a momentous year. Although winter and early spring were quiet on the Western Front, April was to see a major offensive at Arras in which one "Boy" lost his life followed by the assault on Vimy Ridge where the Canadians finally achieved success. On 31 July, the allies launched their 'Push' around Ypres that would become known as Passchendaele and during which a further two "Boys" died. Globally, the revolution in Russia brought the end of the Romanoff dynasty and, under a deal with Germany, Russia left the War which was to have significant consequences for the Allies in 1918. In April 1917 the United States of America entered the war on the Allies side but their impact would not be felt until 1918.

On the sea however, there was little action but the first "Boy" to die in 1917 was in the Royal Navy, the only one of "The Boys" not to serve in the army. **Herbert William Wills** was born on 8 June 1895 in the Barnsbury area of Islington. The family moved to Walthamstow in about 1896 and Herbert was baptised there on 2 May 1897. In 1901 they were living at 7, Shaftesbury Road in the south of Walthamstow and Herbert's father, William was a clerk with a contractor's firm. William and his wife Grace also had four daughters. Herbert joined Blackhorse Road School on 8 January 1906 from Maynard Road School[125] and by then the family was living at 30, Fairfield Road in Higham Hill, Walthamstow. He left school on 30 July 1909, aged 14, and in 1911 he was working as an electrical instruments apprentice. The family were still living at

---

[125] Maynard Road Board School opened in 1884, the predecessor of Henry Maynard School.

30, Fairfield Road and Herbert now had five more siblings. All 10 children survived infancy. They later moved a few roads north to 11, Claremont Road.

On 7 December 1914 Herbert enlisted for 12 years in the Royal Navy. He was working as a junior mechanic with the General Post Office. Herbert was initially based on H.M.S. Pembroke II.[126] From 21 December 1915 until 21 May 1916 he was based on H.M.S. Alert, an Alert-Class sloop which had been lent to the civil authority at Basra in 1906 for use as a pilot vessel. From 22 May 1916 until 27 February 1917 he was based on H.M.S. Dalhousie,[127] a base Guard Ship at Basra. During this period he served as a member of the armourer's crew[128] on H.M.S. Mantis[129] (see Illustrations section) which patrolled the River Tigris. Her role was to support the troops fighting the Ottoman Turks in Mesopotamia, now Iraq.

For centuries, Mesopotamia had been part of the Ottoman Empire but the allies wanted to annex the land to get oil supplies for the navy. Some of the Sheikhs in the area supported the allies, others the Germans and Ottoman Turks. The allied troops deployed in the region were mainly Indian and they met strong Ottoman resistance.

On 24 February 1917 H.M.S. Mantis anchored at Kut-al-Amara to hoist the Union Jack after Kut was recaptured, having been in Ottoman hands since 29th April 1916. Accompanied by other ships, she proceeded beyond Kut and supported the attacks on the

---

[126] HMS Pembroke II was a Royal Navy Shore Station at Eastchurch, Sheppey, Kent. There were Shore Stations around the British coast, all named after ships.
[127] A copy of a painting of H.M.S.Dalhousie at Basra is kept at the Imperial War Museum. It can be viewed at http://www.iwm.org.uk/collections/search?f%5B0%5D=agentString%3ARoyal%20Navy%2C%20DALHOUSIE%20%28HMS%29&query=
[128] The Armourer's Crew looked after the ship's guns and shells.
[129] H.M.S. Mantis was an Insect-class River Gunboat of 645 tons, launched in September 1915. She carried 2 x 6 inch and 2 x 12 pounder guns and a complement of 53 men. H.M.S. Mantis was deployed to patrol the River Tigris from 1 March 1916 to 27 April 1917.

Ottoman Turks as they retreated towards Baghdad. On 26 February 1917 there was heavy firing. The ship's machine guns were in action against hostile Arabs on the river's right bank and there was close action with a large retreating force of Ottoman Turks. Two crew members were killed and two, including Herbert Wills, were severely wounded. Three others were slightly wounded.

The Ship's Log for 27 February 1917 records that at 12.00 Noon. 'Wills, Herbert, Armourers Crew ONM10813 died of wounds.'[130] At 5.30 pm a 'Burial party left ship to bury one rating.' Herbert was buried on the right bank of the River Tigris at Malago Reach, Mesopotamia, now Iraq. He has no known grave and is commemorated on the Basra Memorial.[131] He was 21 years old.

There was also fighting against the Turkish Ottoman Empire in Egypt where the Suez Canal was a vital link in allowing troops and equipment from Australia, New Zealand and India to reach the Western Front, as well as food, minerals and other resources en route to Britain. Frank Mace was serving there prior to being returned to the UK to die in March. Thomas Waller was also to die there.

Francis Edward (Frank) Mace was born on 8 April 1894 in Bethnal Green and was baptised on 29 April at St Thomas's Church, Bethnal Green.[132] The family were living at 23, Cyprus Street and his father, William, was a cook. By 1901 the family were living at 33, Blackhorse Lane, Walthamstow, just round the corner from the school,

---

[130] Log Book, H.M.S. Mantis, 27 February 1917.
[131] The Basra Memorial commemorates more than 40,500 members of the Commonwealth forces who died in the Mesopotamia operations from the Autumn of 1914 to the end of August 1921 and who have no known grave. Until 1997 the Basra Memorial was located on the main quay of Maqil naval dockyard, on the west bank of the Shatt-al-Arab, about 8 kilometres north of Basra. Because of the site's sensitivity it was moved and is located 32 kilometres along the road to Nasiriyah, in the middle of what was a major battleground during the first Gulf War.
[132] St. Thomas's Church, Baroness Road, Bethnal Green. 1848-1951. Damaged by bombing in the Second World War and demolished.

and William was now a dining room manager. William and Mary Ann had two other children and his mother's sister and a nursemaid were also resident. Frank joined Blackhorse Road School on 27 August 1901 from Coppermill School, presumably transferring to his new local school, and left on 25 April 1902 when, aged 8, he left the parish. Given that, in 1911, he was living at 4, St James Street at the bottom of Walthamstow High Street and working as a commercial clerk, it is likely that he moved to a school nearer that address. Number 4 is part of a parade of shops so possibly at that time it was a café or restaurant as his father was now working as a cook. There were three more siblings, including his younger brother George, born in 1902, the future Mayor of Waltham Forest, but one other child had died.

Francis's Service Record indicates he initially served as a Private, Number 130066, in the Royal Army Medical Corps. By 1917 he had been promoted and at the time of his death was serving as a Sergeant, now with the Number 2245, in the $2^{nd}/3^{rd}$ East Anglian Field Ambulance,[133] RAMC.[134] Changing service numbers was not unusual as men were moved to different regiments. The $2^{nd}/3^{rd}$ East Anglian Field Ambulance was part of the 54th (East Anglian) Division. From 2 April 1916, the Division were in Egypt occupying the Southern Section of the Suez Canal defences.

There are no records to show whether Francis was wounded or ill but he was returned to England and hospitalised at the Military

---

[133] The Field Ambulance was not a vehicle. It was a mobile front line medical unit manned by the RAMC. Field Ambulances had special responsibility for the care of casualties of one of the Brigades of a Division and were responsible for establishing and operating the casualty evacuation chain from the front line, through an Advanced Dressing Station (ADS) to the Main Dressing Station (MDS). Each Field Ambulance comprised about 60 men.

[134] RAMC members did not carry weapons or equipment. Some were volunteers, others transferred from other regiments, whilst others with medical training, could be requested to enlist. Irrespective of how they joined, they had to show great courage. Some conscientious objectors served amongst their ranks, especially after the Military Service Act of 1916, preferring to save lives rather than take them.

Hospital, Bethnal Green[135] where he died on 10 March 1917. He is one of the four "Boys" buried in Queen's Road Cemetery, Walthamstow. (See Illustrations section) He is also listed on the Brookwood (United Kingdom 1914-1918) Memorial. On 16 June 1917 a sum of £9.11.0d (£9.55p) outstanding pay was paid to his father and on 26 November 1919, his War Gratuity of £11.0.0d was paid to his father. Francis does not have a CWGC headstone and is buried in the family plot in Queen's Road Cemetery with other members of the family including his younger brother George, who was too young to serve, and who went on to become a solicitor, Mayor of Waltham Forest from 1968-1969, and a Freeman of Walthamstow.

On 9 April 1917, British, Canadian, South African, New Zealand, Newfoundland, and Australian troops attacked the German defences near Arras. There were major gains on the first day, followed by stalemate. The battle cost nearly 160,000 British casualties and about 125,000 German casualties and ended on 16 May. The attack was intended as a diversion for the French Nivelle Offensive, an attack on the German positions along the Chemin des Dames ridge. The 15th battalion fought on the first day taking the German front line trench but were then stalled. Private **Samuel Standcumbe** was reported missing in action on the 9/10 April. The lack of accuracy over the date is understandable given the confusion of battle and his body was never recovered. His death was finally confirmed in a Field Service Memo dated 15 May and reported in the local paper on 15 June.[136]

---

[135] The Bethnal Green Military Hospital took over the Bethnal Green Infirmary in Cambridge Heath Road in 1915 and served military personnel until 1920. The hospital was closed in 1990 and demolished. Only the listed four storey administration block remains.

[136] Walthamstow, Leyton and Chingford Guardian 15 June 1917 p6

Samuel George Standcumbe was born in Walthamstow on 6 December 1897.[137] In 1901 the family were living at 69, Walpole Road, Walthamstow, not far from the school, south of Forest Road. His father, Joseph, was a shoemaker and he and his wife, Caroline, had six other children including eleven year old John. Samuel joined Blackhorse Road School on 11 June 1903 from the Infants' School. The family were now living closer to the school at 32, Farnborough Road. In 1911, he was still at school and another sibling had been born. They had a total of 12 children of whom eight had survived. Samuel left school on 26 November 1911 just before his fourteenth birthday.

Samuel was working as a shoemaker when he enlisted in Stratford, aged 18, on 22 February 1916. He served initially in the reserves in the 14th Battalion, The King's Royal Rifle Corps and was mobilised on 12 June 1916. On 22 December 1916 he joined the 15th Battalion, The Durham Light Infantry. By 1 January 1917, according to his battlefield will in which he left everything to his father, the family were now living at 16, Suffolk Park Road, south of Forest Road.

On the same day as Samuel was declared missing, his elder brother John, aged 29, was also killed in the Battle of Arras. He was serving as 393315, Rifleman John Frank Standcumbe, in the London Regiment, Queen Victoria's Rifles. His body was also never recovered and both brothers are commemorated on the Arras Memorial. John had married Elizabeth Alice Taylor in 1911 and they lived at 14, Eldon Road, Walthamstow.

On 7 September 1917 £2.14.10d (£2.74p) outstanding pay was paid to Samuel's sole legatee, his father Joseph. On 12 September 1917 his personal effects were sent to his father who wrote to the regiment on 15 September to say several items were missing; his watch, signet ring, silver and amber cigarette holder in case, pocket book and purse. Presumably these were in his possession when he

---

[137] The School register states his DOB as 6 December 1895 however his Birth record indicates 1897.

went missing. There is no evidence of a reply. On 13 October 1919, Samuel's £3.0.0. War Gratuity was paid to Joseph. On 4 September 1920, authorisation was given for Samuel's family to receive his Victory and War Medals and they acknowledged receipt on 7 September. His father was sent Samuel's scroll and death plaque[138] on 22 January 1922.

Thomas Waller was born in Bethnal Green on 5 August 1898. In 1901 his family were living at Waterlow Industrial Dwellings, 22, Ainsley Street, Bethnal Green.[139] His father, Thomas, was a railway checker (goods) with the Great Eastern Railway and he and Harriett had four children. By 11 June 1906 the family were living at 25, Pasquier Road, Walthamstow, several roads east of the school, when Thomas joined Blackhorse Road School from the Infants'. He left the school because of illness on 11 November 1909 and was re-admitted on 28 February 1910. There is no final leaving date in the roll book but the 1911 Census reports him as aged 12 and at school. His father was still a checker with the GER and there were now five children. His school leaving date would have been about July 1912 when he was nearly 14.

Thomas served as a Rifleman with the 11th Battalion, The London Regiment (Finsbury Rifles). Having seen service at Gallipoli, the regiment had suffered severe losses when it was evacuated to Egypt in December 1915. It remained in Egypt defending the Suez Canal throughout 1916 and in 1917, as part of the Egyptian Expeditionary Force, it fought in three Battles as the

---

[138] From 1919 over 1,000,000 plaques and scrolls were sent to the next of kin of soldiers, sailors, airmen and a few hundred women who had died as a direct consequence of service in the Great War between 4th August 1914 and 30th April 1919. The circular shape and coin-like appearance led to the nickname the "Dead Man's Penny", the "Death Penny", "Death Plaque" or "Widow's Penny". (See Illustrations section)

[139] Ainsley Street was part the Waterlow Estate, made up of tenement blocks, which was built in the second half of the 19th century south of Bethnal Green Road at the Cambridge Heath Road end.

Allies attempted to take Gaza from the Ottoman Turks. The First Battle of Gaza was fought on 26 March 1917 and resulted in a narrow defeat for the Allies. Having gained re-enforcements, the Allies won the Second Battle, fought from 17-19 April. Thomas however was killed, aged 18, on 19 April and is buried in the Gaza War Cemetery in present day Palestine. After the Third Battle, which started on the morning of 31 October, the Allies finally took Gaza on 9 November. They were able to pursue the retreating Ottoman army and captured Jerusalem on 9 December.

Meanwhile, on the Western Front, a plan had been in place since early 1916 for a major Offensive in the Ypres area but had been diverted by the Somme Offensive of 1916. Having successfully secured the high ground of the Wytschaete-Messines Ridge in the Battle of Messines from 7-14 June, Haig's plan was to advance against the German Front Line east and north-east of Ypres. On reaching the high ground of the Passchendaele Ridge to the north-east of Ypres, the British planned to continue to the west, cutting off German access to the Belgian ports of Ostende and Zeebrugge where German forces were in control and were using Zeebrugge in particular for submarine warfare against allied shipping. Also, a British offensive before the autumn would draw the German Army's attention away from the Aisne region. A large French offensive on the Chemin des Dames Ridge in April 1917 had been a failure with very high casualties and had resulted in some French units mutinying.

The British Fifth Army advanced in a north-easterly direction away from its positions near Ypres with the Passchendaele Ridge in its sights. The French First Army was on its left and The British Second Army on its right, holding the ground won during the Battle of Messines. Approximately two miles was gained on the first day but, that night, rain began to fall and the ground quickly turned into a quagmire. Churned up by the artillery bombardment of the

German Front Line, the ground the British were now having to advance across was badly damaged and filling up with of rainwater which could not drain away through the heavy clay soil. In addition, several small streams flowed through the area and their drainage channels had been destroyed. Because of persistent rain over the next few weeks the whole operation became bogged down in thick, Flanders mud and conditions were so bad that men and horses disappeared into the water-filled craters.

The Germans had fortified their defensive line in expectation of an attack in this area so that the British advance turned into a battle of eight phases, known collectively as the Third Battle of Ypres or Passchendaele, as in the Siegfried Sassoon[140] poem, 'Memorial Tablet',

'I died in hell -
(They called it Passchendaele.)'

Instead of a major assault, the Allies inched closer to the Passchendaele Ridge in a series of actions but now with limited objectives. The first Battle, at Pilckem Ridge, took place between 31 July and 2 August. It was followed between 16-18 August by the Battle of Langemarck. From 20-25 September the Battle of the Menin Road Ridge was fought; from 26 September-3 October the Battle of Polygon Wood; on 4 October the Battle of Broodseinde and on 9 October the Battle of Poelcapelle. The First Battle of Passchendaele was fought on 12 October and the final battle, the Second Battle of Passchendaele was fought between 26 October and 10 November. The capture of Passchendaele Village eventually took over 8 weeks to achieve with huge costs to both sides and estimates of 310,000 Allied and 260,000 German casualities. Exact figures are unknown and many of those casualties were never found and have no known grave. Included amongst the casualties are four "Boys", two of whom were among the lost.

---

[140] Siegfried Sassoon, CBE, MC. 1886-1967. English poet, writer and soldier who served throughout the War.

Harry Wilson was born on 30 August 1889 in Tottenham. By April 1891 the family was living at 3, Lincoln Road, Tottenham, and his father, William was a litho machine worker. He and Jane had two other children. In April 1901 they were living at 55, Herbert Road, Tottenham, with William now described as a litho printer transfer worker and a further child had been born. By 28 August 1901, when Harry joined Blackhorse Road School from Page Green School Tottenham,[141] the family were living at 76, Gloucester Road, Walthamstow, north of the school in Higham Hill. Harry left school on 23 December 1903 aged 14. In April 1911, aged 21, he was a carpenter, living at 10, Renness Road, Walthamstow, just north of Forest Road, with his parents and youngest sibling. There had been seven children of whom three had died. Harry enlisted on 13 October 1916 and served as a Private in the London Regiment (7th City of London).

In 1917, The London Regiment was based in the Ypres region and took part in the attack on Messines Ridge. On 7 June 1917 the Allies launched a major attack on the Wytschaete-Messines ridge aimed at removing the German Army from the high ground south of Ypres which they had held since October 1914. A successful operation would break through the German Front and straighten the British Front Line reducing the manpower needed to man it and improve the Allied position south-east of Ypres. They would then be in a better position to protect the right flank of the large-scale British attack planned for the end of July to the east and north-east of Ypres. To help the attack, from the early spring of 1916 mining operations were carried out to dig tunnels under the German lines and lay explosives for 21 mines. On 7 June, 19 of the 21 mines were blown at 3.10am. 19 enormous craters were left after the debris had crashed down and the noise of the explosions was heard in London. Some 6,000 German troops were killed. The assault on the German line was then carried out by Allied troops. Over 7,000 German prisoners were taken and by the end of the first day the Allied objectives had been achieved. On

---

[141] Page Green Board School opened in Broad Lane in 1882.

that day however, Harry Wilson, aged 27, was killed. He is buried in Voormezeele Enclosure, No. 3 on the Ieper to Kemmel road. His body would have been brought there from an outlying cemetery after the Armistice.

Arthur William Wiles was born in Bedford on 8 May 1892. The family moved to Walthamstow between 1895-1899 and in 1901 they were living at 2, Cross Street.[142] Arthur's parents, Charles and Mary also had two daughters. Charles was a railway signalman and they had two boarders, both railway signalmen, living in the house. Arthur joined Blackhorse Road School on 2 December 1901 from Pretoria Avenue Infants.[143] No leaving date is given but it would have been April or May 1906 when he was aged 14. By 1911, aged 16, he was still at the same address with his parents and two siblings and working as an apprentice French polisher. His father was working for the Midland railway as a signalman.

Arthur served as a Gunner in 'B' Battery, 107th Brigade, The Royal Field Artillery (RFA). This brigade served with 24th Division and had been established in September 1914 as part of Kitchener's Third New Army. The RFA was reasonably mobile being moved wherever there was a need and was responsible for the medium calibre guns and howitzers deployed close to the front line. In April 1917 the 107th was in action at Vimy Ridge and in June fought at Messines. Arthur was wounded and it is likely he was taken to the 10th Casualty Clearing Station (CCS) at Remy Sidings, Lijssenthoek[144] where he died of his wounds on 15 June 1917, aged 25. He is buried in Lijssenthoek Military Cemetery.[145]

---

[142] Now demolished, Cross Street was a turning off Pretoria Avenue.
[143] Pretoria Avenue Board School opened in 1888 and closed in 1938.
[144] Information on the Lijssenthoek Visitors Centre can be found at http://www.lijssenthoek.be/index.php
[145] Lijssenthoek Military Cemetery is the second largest Commonwealth War Cemetery in Belgium and is located between Ypres and Poperinge. Remy Sidings CCS was situated on the main communication line between the Allied military bases in the rear and the channel and the Ypres battlefields. A railway line existed then.

Arthur's death was reported in the local paper on 6 July[146] and 3 August.[147] A payment of £12.17.11d (£12.90p) was made to his mother on 24 November 1917 and on 22 December 1919 his War Gratuity of £13.0.0d was paid to his father.

Three of "The Boys" received medals for gallantry. The first of these was **James Alfred Vickery** who was born in Walthamstow on 17 October 1897. In 1901 he was living at 16, Russell Road, Walthamstow, off Forest Road, with his parents, Robert and Caroline, and five older siblings. His father was a pensioned police constable. Robert's brother and three boarders were also living in the house. James joined Blackhorse Road School on 3 April 1905 from the Infants' School by which time they were living at 8, Pasquier Road. In 1911 they were still living at that address, with four of the other siblings. James left school on 15 November 1911 aged 14. His father died, aged 61, in 1914.

When he enlisted in Stratford, James was working for the Post Office at the GPO Eastern District Office in the Whitechapel Road.[148] His name is on their War Memorial with details of his gallantry. James went to France on 11 August 1915 to join the 7th (Service) Battalion Seaforth Highlanders (Rossshire Buffs). The 7th Battalion was raised at Fort George in August 1914 as part of Kitchener's First New Army and joined 26th Brigade in the 9th (Scottish) Division. The Seaforth Highlanders was a kilted regiment and it is not clear why James was with a Scottish Regiment however possible reasons include him knowing someone already in the regiment; the regiment recruiting in London at the time James wanted to enlist – at that time they were stationed on Salisbury Plain; being allocated to infill for casualties or, the attraction of the kilt. The regimental museum reports that women found the kilt attractive encouraging men to enlist as a result.

The 7ths were part of the 9th (Scottish) Division at the Battle of Loos from 25 September–14 October 1915 and were charged to

---
[146] Walthamstow, Leyton and Chingford Guardian 6 July 1917 p6
[147] Walthamstow, Leyton and Chingford Guardian 3 August 1917 p6
[148] see http://www.62316.mrsite.com/page23.htm

attack the well defended Hohenzollern Redoubt and Fosse 8, the high location of the main enemy observation posts looking across the whole battlefield. Although they made good initial progress, they were halted by the Germans who launched a counter attack which included gas. A further attack saw heavy losses for no gain. The Battle of Loos continued until 14 October and resulted in over 61,000 British casualties of whom 7,766 were killed. Casualties were particularly high among Scots units and the 9th (Scottish) Division suffered 6,058 of whom 190 were officers including their Commanding Officer, G. H. Thesiger and the Commanding Officer of the 7th Seaforths, Lieutenant-Colonel W. Gaisford. On the third day of the battle, 27 September, James carried out the act of gallantry for which he was to be recommended for the Distinguished Conduct Medal.[149]

During early 1916, James was promoted to Lance Corporal and in June 1916 he was awarded the DCM. The London Gazette stated 'VICKERY, James A. DCM, S/8224 4th Bn Seaforth Highlanders For conspicuous gallantry. At a critical moment L/Cpl Vickery and CQMS[150] Beech steadied the men by getting up on the parapet and playing tunes on mouth organs, although exposed to a heavy fire.'[151]

The mouth organ incident caused James to make the national press as, on Friday 24 June 1916, the Daily Express ran an article headlined

GOLD MOUTH-ORGAN FOR A D.C.M.
HOW CHEERY FUNDERS WILL HONOUR TWO BRAVE MEN.
'DESPISED INSTRUMENT'
SEAFORTHS RALLIED AT A CRITICAL TIME

---

[149] The Distinguished Conduct Medal was instigated to recognise acts of gallantry performed by 'other ranks' (i.e. NCOs) during the Crimean War and was regarded as second only to the Victoria Cross in prestige. Because of concern that the greater demand for medals during the Great War would devalue the prestige of those already available, the Military Medal was issued as an alternative to the DCM from March 1916. Although the DCM was still available the MM was usually awarded other than for exceptional acts of bravery.

[150] CQMS – Company Quartermaster Sergeant.

[151] London Gazette 21 June 1916 p 6157

The War Memorial in the old school hall in Clifton Avenue, prior to it being placed in the new school foyer

Map showing the streets around the school in 1913
The three departments of the school can be clearly seen with the industrial works north of the Royal Standard on Blackhorse Lane. Blackhorse Road Station is on the opposite side of Blackhorse Lane to its present position and the lines of the old goods yard, where the new Willowfield Humanities College stands, can be seen.

The Blackhorse Road Schools' site in the early 1960s
The three departments of Blackhorse Road School just prior to the Clifton Avenue block being demolished for the Willowfield School playground. The other two blocks were integrated in to the new school and a new block built on the building site in the foreground. Compare the photograph with the map. The site is bounded by Clifton Avenue, now fully built, which runs North West to South East at the left of the photograph and which lost two "Boys"; Blackhorse Lane which runs West to North East towards the top; Tavistock Avenue which runs North West to South East at the right of the photo, which also saw two "Boys" killed and Pembar Avenue which runs North East to South West at the bottom right of the photograph. The parallel road to Tavistock Avenue going North East is Blenheim Road which lost seven "Boys", the most of any street.

The two remaining 'departments', the Boys' School and, beyond it, the Girls' School, on Tavistock Avenue in 2015

The Boys' Department in 2015

The school hall from the 1901 building still in use when the school moved to its new site in 2015

One of classrooms from the 1901 building still in use when the school moved to its new site in 2015

Clifton Avenue houses, opposite the school, in 2015 showing some of their original features "The Boys" would have seen. The houses are typical of many in the area around the school. Percy Spreadborough lived at number 27, the house on the left.

August 1914. Volunteers waiting to enlist

Several of "The Boys" served as Gunners

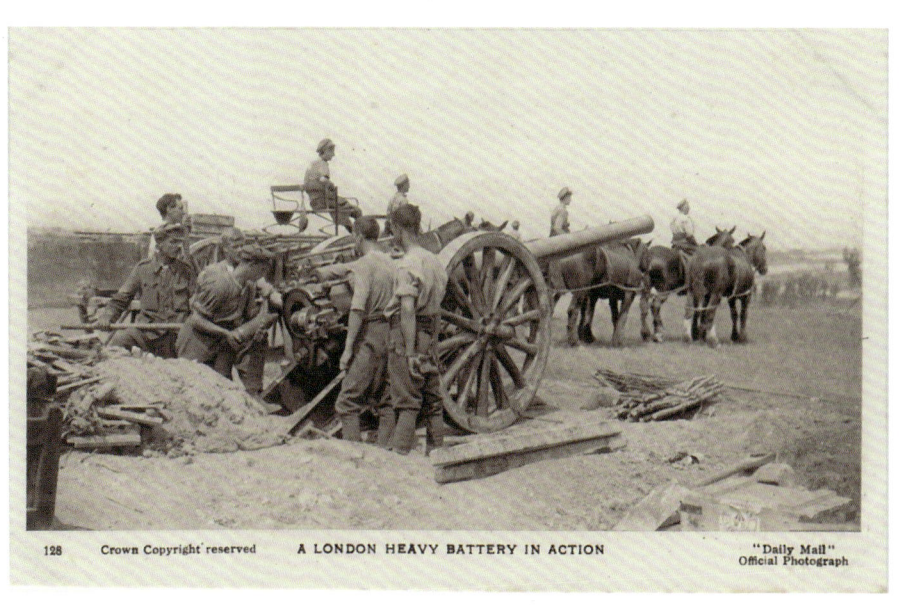

*The heavy guns were moved by horse power
requiring experienced riders*

H. M. S. Mantis. Herbert Wills' ship.

A Sergeant in the Seaforth Highlanders, the regiment in which James Vickery served

James Vickery's mouth organ, presented by readers of the Daily Express, displayed in The Highlanders' Museum

James Vickery's medals on display in The Highlanders' Museum

The DCM and the three medals known as 'Pip, Squeak and Wilfred'. "The Boys" who served in 1914-1915 were awarded the 1914-1915 Star. Some may have been awarded the 1914 Star. These were known as 'Pip'. The British Victory Medal, awarded to combatants who served between 5 August 1914 and 11 November 1918, was known as 'Squeak'. The Allied Victory Medal, known as 'Wilfred', was awarded by individual countries and was inscribed on the rim with the recipient's name. Usually, all recipients of 'Wilfred' received 'Squeak' and all recipients of 'Pip' also received 'Squeak' and 'Wilfred'.

Royal Army Medical Staff in action

Two of "The Boys" served in the RAMC bringing back the wounded from the battlefields to Casualty Clearing Stations. RAMC were unarmed but nevertheless had to experience extreme danger.

Casualties after the battle

*"The Boys" would have experienced the moment before an attack.
The devastation caused by shelling can be clearly seen.*

Troops following up an initial attack. A stretcher bearer can be seen walking out to recover the wounded.

The Silver War Badge

Ernest Nottage would have been awarded one of these when he was discharged. It was made of Sterling silver and was worn on the right breast of the person's civilian clothing. It could not be worn on a military uniform. About 1,150,000 Silver War Badges were issued in total for First World War service.

The families of service personnel killed in action received the 'Death Penny' and scroll and a letter from the King. This one was sent to the parents of the author's Great-Uncle, Ernest Sharp who was killed in action in April 1918, aged 20.

The Menin Gate entrance to Ypres during the War

The Menin Gate Memorial

A section of the Menin Gate showing some of the 54,000 names of men who died in the area and have no known grave. Three "Boys" are commemorated here.

Aubrey Cox's grave. He does not have a CWGC headstone and is buried with his parents who both pre-deceased him.

Francis Mace does not have a CWGC headstone and is buried in the family tomb.

Ernest Nottage's CWGC headstone has been incorporated into the family grave which also contains both his parents.

George Mills' headstone with the added tribute to his brother.

The graves of the four "Boys" buried in Queen's Road Cemetery

Louis Simmonds' grave in the Südfriedhof Cemetery, Cologne

The Thiepval Memorial to the Missing of the Somme. Eight of "The Boys" are commemorated here.

The Daily Express had a scheme called the 'Cheery Chums' which raised money to send gifts to the troops. Included amongst the parcels were mouth organs or 'm-os' as our soldiers call them' and goes on to suggest the mouth organ James played was one sent by the newspaper noting with surprise that 'one of them would be the direct means of steadying men at a critical moment and earning a D.C.M. for the quick-witted gallant hero who played it.'[152] The writer, under the penname Orion, continues

> 'I went to our stock-room immediately and chose two of the very best-toned mouth-organs from among the thousands we have. I removed the top and bottom nickel plates. In their place I propose to have placed two real gold plates. These will be inscribed with a short account of the heroic deed that inspired the gift, and when they have been slipped into a lined morocco leather case, they will be sent to C.Q.M.S. Beech and Lance-Corporal Vickery as a present from Cheery Funders.'[153]

The mouth organs must have been delivered as James's gold mouth organ, suitably inscribed, is in the possession of The Highlanders' Museum[154] in Fort George, Inverness. (See illustrations section) The Daily Express carried further articles on the 24, 26 and 28 June. On Saturday 26, Orion wished 'that Mr. Rudyard Kipling[155] would immortalise this feat of mouth-organry which has won the D.C.M. for Beech and mention for Vickery.'[156] Money continued to be raised for the Mouth Organs and on Monday 26, Orion argued for an all British mouth organ

---

[152] Daily Express 23 June 1916 p2
[153] Ibid
[154] The Highlanders' Museum houses The Seaforth's records.
[155] Rudyard Kipling, 1865-1932. Poet and writer. His only son, John was killed at Loos. He chose "Their Name Liveth For Evermore" on Stones of Remembrance and "Known unto God" on the gravestones of unknown soldiers.
[156] Daily Express 24 June 1916 p2

despite the manufacturing problems this involved.[157] The gold mouth organ was duly presented, although there is no record of where, but perhaps it was when James was next home on leave.

In 1916 the regiment was in action in the Battle of the Somme, including the capture of Longueval, the Battle of Delville Wood and the Battle of Le Transloy.

According to the School Log Book, on 15 February 1917 whilst home on leave, 'Lance-Corporal James Vickery D.C.M. called today to see the old school'.[158] It is not difficult to imagine the excitement and pride of the war hero visiting the school and presumably showing his medal to the pupils and possibly playing his mouth organ.

From 9 April-16 May the regiment took part in the First and Second Battles of the Scarpe during the Battle of Arras. The regiment was then moved to Belgium to take part in the Big Push that was to be Third Ypres and between 31 July and 2 August they fought in the Battle of Pilkem Ridge.

On 13 September, seven months after visiting his old school, James Vickery, D.C.M. was reported missing, presumed killed. According to the 7th Seaforth Highlanders' War Diary, the battalion was out of the line at that time and had been so for some weeks. The only casualties recorded in the War Diary for that day were 2nd Lieutenant Holmes (football accident) and two OR's[159] 'sick to Field Ambulance'.

At that time, the offensive which would become known as the Battle of the Menin Road, had begun on 31 August with an artillery bombardment which intensified from 13 September. A few small scale raids were carried out during this time however there were over 10,000 Allied casualties, mainly at the hands of the German guns.

---

[157] The shortage of mouth organs was because, prior to the war, they were only produced in Germany and the supply ceased early in the war. Inferior ones were produced in Switzerland but that supply also dried up.
[158] School Log Book 15 February 1917
[159] Other Ranks.

So therein lies a mystery as, if the regiment was not involved in action, how did James die? His body was never found, possibly having been buried and the location lost when further action took place in the area, or possibly it was so badly damaged it was impossible to identify him. He has no known grave and is commemorated on the Tyne Cot Memorial[160] near Ypres. His death was reported in the local paper on 29 September.[161]

On 5 February 1919 sums of £5.17.8d (£5.87p) from his outstanding pay were paid to each of his mother, Caroline, and his sisters, Lillian Thomas, Mabel Smith and Amy Garroway. On 3 April 1919, at the request of his brother Robert, a further sum of £5.17.8d (£5.88p) was paid to Winifred A Vickery. This provides a further mystery as we have no information as to how she was related to James and why she was entitled to an equal share. It may well be that this was a stipulation in his battlefield will but she was not his wife as his mother was his next of kin and on 12 December 1919 James's War Gratuity of £11.10.0d (£11.50p) was paid to her. She was now living at 2, Renness Road, Walthamstow. James was awarded the 1915 Star as a Private and the Victory and War Medals as a Lance-Corporal.

On 31 August 1985, his medals and mouth organ were donated to The Highlanders' Museum by his nephew, Mr E. J. Garroway, the son of his sister Amy.

The final "Boy" to die in 1917 was **Henry John Lowings**. He was born on 25 March 1890 in Tottenham and was baptised

---

[160] Tyne Cot Cemetery and Memorial is named after 'Tyne Cot' or 'Tyne Cottage', the name given by the Northumberland Fusiliers to a barn which stood nearby. Initially it was an Advanced Dressing Station cemetery and was greatly enlarged after the Armistice when remains were brought in from the battlefields of Passchendaele and Langemarck, and from a few small burial grounds. It is the largest Commonwealth war cemetery in the world with 11,956 Commonwealth servicemen of the First World War buried or commemorated, 8,369 of whom are unidentified.

[161] Walthamstow, Leyton and Chingford Guardian 29 September 1917 p4

on 15 June at St John's Church, Stamford Hill.[162] In 1891 he was living at 31, Albert Road, Tottenham, off the Seven Sisters Road, with his parents Henry J, a commercial clerk, and Louisa and his younger sibling William. There were two further children before Louisa died, aged 36, in 1899. Henry senior remarried on 11 March 1900 to Ruth Elizabeth Meadows, aged 24, at Holy Trinity Church, Tottenham.[163] In 1901 they were living at 63, Westerfield Road, Tottenham, near Seven Sisters Station, and Henry senior was now a poultry shopkeeper.

By the time Henry joined Blackhorse Road School on 2 September 1901 he had attended at least two other schools. Named as John Henry, he was admitted to Campbell Street School,[164] Maida Vale, and Westminster on 18 June 1894. The family address was now 7, Maida Vale and his father's occupation was given as poulterer. When he joined Blackhorse Road School, Henry was attending Earlsmead School, Tottenham.[165] The family were now living at 33, Clarence Road, Walthamstow, north of the school off Blackhorse Lane. He remained at Blackhorse Road School until 14 March 1904 when he left, shortly before his fourteenth birthday. In 1911 he was 21 and working as a pork butcher and the family now lived at 80, Fulbourne Road, Walthamstow. His father was a poultry salesman and there were now three children of the second marriage.

Given his age, it is possible that Henry was a conscript. He would have been 26 in 1916 when conscription was introduced.[166]

---

[162] St John's Church, Stamford Hill 1886-1975. Now demolished.
[163] Holy Trinity Church, Philip Lane, Tottenham, built 1828-1830, and still functioning as a church.
[164] Campbell Street School, Maida Vale. Opened in 1881 as a Board school for boys, girls and infants. Re-named Paddington Green Primary in 1962 and still functioning as a primary school.
[165] Earlsmead School, Broad Lane, opened 1897. Still exists under same name.
[166] The Military Service Act of March 1916 imposed conscription on single men between 18 and 41 with some exemptions including the unfit, certain industrial workers, clergy and teachers. In May 1916 married men were included.

Henry served with the 8th Battalion, The East Surrey Regiment and was promoted to Lance Corporal. Without his service record it is impossible to know when he joined the regiment and therefore what action he saw. The 8th Battalion, East Surrey Regiment was raised in September 1914 as part of Kitchener's Second New Army and went to France in July 1915. In 1916 they were in action on The Somme at the Battles of Albert, Bazentin Ridge, including the capture of Trones Wood, Delville Wood, Thiepval Ridge, Ancre Heights and the Battle of the Ancre.

In 1917 they took part in the Operations on the Ancre and fought during the German retreat to the Hindenburg Line and in the Third Battle of the Scarpe before moving to Flanders where they saw action in the Battle of Pilckem Ridge, the Battle of Langemarck and the First Battle of Passchendaele[167] where it is likely, on 12 October, that Henry was killed. He has no known grave and is also commemorated on the Tyne Cot Memorial. He was 27.

By the end of 1917, the war had been going for over three years and people at home had become increasingly involved. Not only were the casualties affecting more and more families, the war had reached the British mainland with the increasing threat from the air. At the start of the war, Britain was not prepared for any attack from the air and its defences were focussed on defending the coastline from sea invasion. The Royal Flying Corps (RFC) was deployed overseas with few aircraft available to defend the mainland.

The first air raid had taken place on 21 December 1914 when two bombs were dropped into the sea near the Admiralty Pier in Dover. The Kaiser had ordered that London should not be bombed fearing

---

[167] The First Battle of Passchendaele on 12 October, was part of the Allied attempt to gain ground around Passchendaele however heavy rain and mud made movement difficult and little artillery could be brought close to the front. After a modest British advance, German counter-attacks recovered most of the ground lost opposite Passchendaele. There were 13,000 Allied casualties.

his relatives in the British royal family might be injured. The first successful raid took place on the night of 19–20 January 1915 when two Zeppelins targeted Humberside. Strong winds caused them to be diverted and they dropped their bombs on Great Yarmouth, Sheringham, King's Lynn and the surrounding villages. There were four deaths and 16 people were injured. An order to target the London docks, but not to bomb central London, was agreed by the Kaiser on 5 May. However, because of the lack of accuracy in bombing and the height of the airships, this was always likely to prove difficult. On 30 May, the air attacks came close to the school when 120 bombs were dropped on Stoke Newington, Stepney and Leytonstone and seven people were killed and 35 injured. Further raids were carried out, mainly on coastal towns, and on 17–18 August bombs were dropped on Walthamstow and Leytonstone and 10 people were killed and 48 injured.

In 1915, there were 20 raids. The following year, despite strengthened defences, there were 23 raids which killed 293 and injured 691 people. Several were on London including on 23–24 September when 10 bombs were dropped on Leyton, killing eight people and injuring 30.

The first Gotha aircraft raids took place in March 1917 and on 13 June the first daylight raid on London took place. Mr Simpson recorded it in the School Log Book.

> 'Air raids over London this morning, bombs and guns distinctly heard. A few lads, where parents called, were allowed to go home.'[168]

The consequences that day were very severe with 162 deaths and 432 injuries. Amongst the dead were 16 children killed by a bomb falling on North Street Primary School in Poplar. The following day Mr Simpson recorded that he had

> 'Much trouble from mothers this morning, who were agitated by rumours of raiders. No child left school. This afternoon a detachment of St John's Amb. (Ambulance

---

[168] Boys' School Log Book 13 June 1917

Brigade) occupied the Hall having received notice of Air Raids. All children whose parents called were allowed to go home. Notice came that all was clear at 4 p.m. and the remaining lads went home.'[169]

With continuing night time raids, there were reports of up to 300,000 people seeking shelter in Underground stations and others leaving London to sleep in whatever accommodation was available, some even sleeping in open fields. The air raids were to continue until 5 August 1918 and the people of Walthamstow would have become used to the sight and sound of aircraft and of the defensive guns firing at them. There were locally based airfields from 1915-1918 at Hainault Farm, Suttons Farm and North Weald Bassett to provide cover for the eastern approaches to London.

Food supplies were targetted for the fighting forces in all combatant countries causing shortages for the civilian population. To alleviate the problem, rationing was introduced with Britain introducing it in London early in 1918 and extending it nationwide by the summer.

Internationally, there had been changes in the combatant nations. In Russia, the revolution against the Tsar's regime saw him abdicate on 15 March and on 22 March, the Allies recognised the new Provisional Government. On 6 April the United States declared war on Germany. Despite a strong desire to remain neutral, the loss of life in the sinking of the 'Lusitania'[170] on 7 May 1915 by a German 'U' boat with the loss of 1,198 lives, including 120 Americans, had turned public opinion against Germany. On 13 November the Bolsheviks took power in Russia and from 8 December the Russians ceased fighting the Germans. On 17 December an Armistice was signed

---

[169] Boys' School Log Book 14 June 1917
[170] R.M.S. Lusitania was a Cunard owned British ocean liner and holder of the Blue Riband for the fastest Atlantic crossing. Launched in 1906, she had made 202 trans-Atlantic crossings.

between Russia and Germany at Brest-Litovsk which allowed the Germans to re-deploy their Eastern forces to the Western Front. This was to have serious consequences for the Allies in the spring of 1918.

Chapter 5

1918

Ernest Nottage, Frederick Shea, Alfred Smith, Edward Rollings, Archibald Smith, Joseph Pooley, Ernest Harvey, Flemming Goddard, George Allen, Frederick Keen, John Blackmore, William Peachey, Leslie Conway, Reginald Sellers, Jarvis Engley, Albert Smither, Robert Tresadern, Sydney Bartram, Alfred Cox, Sidney Day, Albert Mills, Cecil French, Louis Simmonds, George Mills

When 1918 dawned there seemed little prospect of peace. The year, however, did see the end of the War but not before 24 more "Boys" had perished.

The first "Boy" to die in 1918 was actually a casualty of injuries received at the Somme eighteen months earlier. **Ernest Harry Nottage** was born in Walthamstow on 9 May 1898.[171] In 1901 he was living at 102, Longfellow Road, Walthamstow, a little way south of Walthamstow Cemetery in Queens Road, with his parents, Thomas and Alice, and a younger sibling. Thomas is described in the Census as a Navvy.[172] There were also two boarders living in the house. On 3 April 1905, Ernest joined Blackhorse Road School from the Infants'. The family had moved to 40, Russell Road, off Forest Road. In 1911 he was still

---

[171] The School On roll register gives his DOB as 9 May 1895 but this must be an error as he was still at school in April 1911 when he would have been 16. Also, he joined from the Infants' School and an 1895 birth would have meant he was nearly 10. 1898 is more likely however see enlistment age. He is noted as aged 3 on the 1901 Census return and 13 on the 1911 Census.

[172] A navvy was a labourer usually employed in road or railway building. Navvy is an abbreviation of navigator, a term used to describe the workers who dug the English canals or navigations.

at school and the family had moved again, this time further south to 62, Erskine Road. His father was now described, more politely, as a General Labourer and his mother as a Blouse Machinist. There were also two more siblings, all at school.

Ernest enlisted on 29 September 1914 at 112, Shaftesbury Street, City Road.[173] He claimed to be 19 years and five months old rather than 16 years and five months but that would fit with the age in the school on-roll record. He is noted in the local newspaper article of Blackhorse Road ex-pupils who had enlisted by November 1914.[174] He was working as an electrical engineer's assistant at the electrical installation, Vurnival Street, London.[175]

Ernest was part of the Home Expeditionary Force until 22 December 1914 when he embarked as a Private with the 2/4 Battalion, The London Regiment, Royal Fusiliers from Southampton on 23 December the *H.M.S. Avon*[176] for Malta, where he disembarked on 2 January 1915. On 20 August 1915 he sailed from Malta for Alexandria, Egypt on the *H.M.T. Southland*[177] disembarking on 24 August for training before sailing for the Dardenelles and Gallipoli on the *H.M.T. Karoo*[178] on 8 October. On 27 October 1915 he received a slight wound to the head but returned to duty the same day.

---

[173] 112, Shaftesbury Street, City Road, a Drill Hall and recruiting station for the London Regiment

[174] Walthamstow, Leyton and Chingford Guardian 20 November 1914 p8

[175] There is no record of a Vurnival Street. There is a Furnival Street off Holborn

[176] H.M.S. Avon, a 'C' class destroyer. Part of the Home and Atlantic Fleet.

[177] H.M.T. Southland was a trans-Atlantic steamer requisitioned as a troopship in 1915. On 2 November 1915 she was torpedoed in the Aegean Sea but was taken in to port and repaired. On 4 June 1917 she was torpedoed off the Irish coast and sank.

[178] H.M.T. Karoo. Australian troopship used for transport duties in the Dardenelles.

The regiment was withdrawn from Gallipoli on 12 December stopping at Mudros[179] before returning to Alexandria on the *'Ionian'*[180] on 22 January 1916. On 17 April 1916 he left Alexandria and sailed to France. He landed at Marseilles on 24 April 1916 and on 6 May he travelled over land to join his new unit in the field, E Company, 1st/4th Battalion, The London Regiment (Royal Fusiliers) on 7 May 1916. On 1 July 1916 they were part of the Allied attack at The Somme, where he was severely wounded. He was treated at the front for wounds to his eye, nose and back on 2 and 3 July before being returned to England on 7 July. He was taken to The Southern General Hospital Headquarters, Edgbaston, Birmingham[181] and the doctor's report, in Ernest's Discharge Documents, written on 19 March 1917 states that on 1 July 1916

> 'while advancing on the Germans (at Huberturne), he was struck in the left cheek by an explosive bullet which destroyed the left eye and shattered the bones at the root of his nose. Another piece of shell entered the right side of the back. The metal in the back was removed in France and the wound healed. He arrived at this hospital on July 9. The patient had considerable cough and the back wound came open again but he never had a tube in. TB was looked for and not found. The face wound healed of its own but the eye was completely destroyed.'

In pen someone has added 'The wound at back was followed by emphysema which is still discharging.'

In the light of his injuries, Ernest was no longer fit for service. Knowing this, on 19 March 1917 he applied for munitions work using his pre-war experience as an electrical engineer's assistant as

---

[179] Port on the Greek island of Lemnos used as a base for the attacks on the Dardenelles.
[180] S.S. Ionian, Canadian defensively armed merchant ship (DEMS) sunk 20 October 1917 off the Pembrokeshire coast.
[181] In August 1914, the University Of Birmingham buildings were taken over by the military authorities as the 1st Southern General Hospital. The whole of the site was converted into a hospital which treated over 64,000 patients during the War.

evidence of his suitability.

A further report on 22 March for the Medical Board states that 'The face wound is healed. The root of the nose is quite depressed giving the saddle nose appearance. The left eye is entirely gone. There is a hole in the nasal septum and the patient cannot get air through the upper passages of the left side of the nose. The back wound is discharging a little and the patient is very short of breath.'

The report adds that he should be
'discharged for further military service. Recommend for sanatorium treatment.'

On 22 March 1917 it was confirmed that he was no longer physically fit for war service. He applied for his discharge from the service and this was granted on 4 April 1917. He was awarded a weekly pension of 27/6 (£1.37 1/2p) the equivalent of £85.50 today, conditional for 26 weeks. With wartime inflation increasing the price of basic goods such as meat, milk and butter by 100% between 1914 and 1918, this was not a large sum to live on.

On his Service Record, 'His Military Character' was reported as 'Very Good' and 'His Character awarded in accordance with King's Regulations' states 'This man has a very good character.' His discharge was confirmed on 12 April 1917, Ernest having served 2 years and 196 days, and he was awarded the Silver Badge, number 157,847, to wear on his tunic as a discharged soldier. (See Illustrations section) The Service Record has Henry typed as his second name, corrected in pen, to Harry.

We do not know if Ernest got munitions work and, sadly, he did not survive for long, dying in University College Hospital in central London on 6 January 1918. His death certificate records that he died, aged 20, of 'Emphysema 9 months' and 'Broncho pneumonia'. Ernest is buried in Queen's Road Cemetery, Walthamstow and his parents added 'Sleeping. His soul now rests in peace that comes of a duty well done' to his headstone. Ernest's CWGC headstone has been incorporated into the family grave which also contains the remains of his mother and father. (See Illustrations section)

On 30 November 1918 his discharge certificate was sent to his mother and on 2 December 1918 his mother signed to acknowledge receipt. On 3 May 1920 his War Gratuity of £11.10s.0d (£11.50) was awarded to his father. Ernest's mother was sent his 1914-1915 Star and the British Victory Medal on 12 August 1920 and on 6 April 1921 his Pension was awarded.

The first "Boy" to be killed in 1918 was **Frederick David Shea.** Like his younger brother George who died at the Somme in 1916, Frederick's history is interesting. The family lived separately and collectively at eight different addresses in south, central and east London between 1889 and 1911 with a further mystery after he was killed.

Frederick was born in Camberwell on 6 February 1889. In 1891 on Census Day he was living at 299, Strand, just around the corner from Waterloo Bridge, with his maternal grandmother, Amelia Coutirier, 56, a widow and hairdresser, Louis Francis, her son, aged 27, a bookseller, Frances Shea, her daughter aged 29, and Frederick's three siblings. The household also contained a servant and a friend. Ten year later he was a 12 year old schoolboy, living with his maternal grandmother, Amelia Coutirier, 67, now described as a Clapham-born bookseller, at 209, Clapham Road, a substantial property near Stockwell Station, his uncle, Francis L. Coutirier, described as a "bookseller's assistant", and his younger brother, George, 14, who had been born in Manor Park, Essex. The 1901 Census showed his mother, Frances, aged 39, housekeeper and three other children, living at 14, Holywell Street, St Clement Danes, Strand.[182]

[182] Holywell Street ran parallel to the Strand between the churches of St Clement Dane and St Mary-le-Strand. Demolished in 1902-03 when the Aldwych was created, it is now covered by the block including Bush House and the Australian High Commission. It retained some of its Elizabethan overhanging frontages. In the 19th Century it was famous for radical pamphlets, booksellers and printing but by the later part of the century it had become disreputable, being more renowned for pornography.

Frederick joined Blackhorse Road School on 23 July 1902 from Stockwell National School. His father, George, was noted as living at 16, Tavistock Avenue, Walthamstow, the same road as the school. Frederick left school on 17 February 1903 aged 14. In 1911, aged 22, he was working as clerk in a grocery warehouse, and living at 425, Forest Road, Walthamstow, with his mother, noted as a widow of private means aged 49, and two of his siblings including his brother, George. Four of the children were living but three others were deceased. Intriguing as it is, it has not been possible to trace George senior or to establish why the family moved so frequently and were often split up.

Frederick enlisted in Lambeth on 25 November 1915. Early in 1916 he married Mabel Alice Cowles. Mabel had been born in Leytonstone in 1892 and in 1901 was living at 93, Blackhorse Road, Walthamstow, so she may have attended Blackhorse Road Girls' School. In 1911 her family were living at 121, Winchester Road, Higham Hill and Mabel, aged 19, was working as a battery maker at the Xylonite factory in Highams Park.

We have no information on Frederick's war service but the 11th Battalion, The Queen's (Royal West Surrey Regt.) was a Service Battalion made up of mainly Kitchener Volunteers so it is likely Frederick served with them throughout his service. The regiment was sent to France on 5 May 1916 and took part in the Battles of Flers-Courcelette from 15-22 September and Transloy Ridge from 1-8 October. On 6 September 1916, Frederick's brother George was killed in the Somme region.

Frederick's regiment was sent to Belgium and served in the Ypres area taking part in the Battle of Messines, the Battle of Pilckem Ridge, the Battle of the Menin Road and operations on the Flanders coast. In November 1917, the regiment was deployed to Italy to strengthen the Italian resistance against the Germans and Austro-Hungarians after the Italian defeat at Caporetto. The Italians had been forced back 12 miles and suffered heavy casualties.

On December 4 1917 the XIth and XIVth British Corps took

over the Montello sector of the River Piave Front. No major battles were fought, however there were raids on enemy held objectives. Frederick was a Lance Corporal, unpaid,[183] when he was killed on 19 January 1918. He is buried in the Giavara British Cemetery, Italy.

There is a further final mystery about Frederick Shea. On 13 April 1918 payment of £8.0.10d (£8.4p) outstanding wages was made to his legatee, Mabel and on 2 December 1919 his War Gratuity of £9.0.0 was also paid to her. According to his military record he had been living in Stockwell when he served however, nearly thirty years after his death, on 20 January 1947, probate on the estate of Frederick David Shea of 121, Winchester Road, Higham's Park, who died on war service on 18 January 1918, was granted to Mabel Alice Burnett, (wife of Alexander Irvine Burnett). The effects were worth £573.9.5d (£573.47 1/2p). 121, Winchester Road had been Mabel's home in 1911. Mabel A Shea had married Alexander Burnett at St George's Hanover Square, London in the summer of 1922. Having been named as his legatee, even though she had married someone else, she remained his heir. Why, therefore did it take 30 years for probate to be granted on his estate and, was the significant sum of £573.9.5d the value the property had increased to by 1947? Had he become the owner of the property when he married Mabel in 1916 and, if so, what happened to her family? Did Mabel continue to live there after Frederick's death and where did she live after she married Alexander? If they did not live in the house, who lived there until January 1947? Unfortunately, we will probably never know.

Alfred William Smith was born in Whitechapel on 17 July 1892. The family moved to Walthamstow before 1895 and in 1901

---

[183] Lance-Corporal is the lowest NCO rank. It could be given and withdrawn by the Commanding Officer but removing more senior ranks from a soldier required a Court Martial. Soldiers sometimes took on the additional responsibility on a probationary basis or on a temporary basis. Units were limited by Establishment as to how many paid Lance Corporals they could have. They could have unlimited unpaid L/Corporals.

were living at 33, Higham Hill Road with father, Alfred, a map mounter, mother, Fannie, a dress maker, and six other siblings. The family had previously lived in Birmingham. Alfred joined Blackhorse Road School when it opened on 28 August 1901 from Higham Hill School and was taken off roll on 25 May 1906, shortly before he was 14. Whilst at school, he took the Labour exams. At that time some pupils, at the discretion of the school, were entered for examinations to see if they could get a scholarship. As we have already seen, getting a scholarship did not guarantee a place in a Higher Elementary School as there were additional costs to be met by the family such as uniform. Alfred's father having died, aged 45, in 1904 would have meant he needed to leave school to support the family.

In 1911 aged 18, Alfred is noted as a stepson and was working as a clerk and living at 4, Orchard Street,[184] with his mother, his married older sister, two brothers, of whom one is also named as a step son, and two unrelated children, Thomas Moorcroft, aged 7 and Winifred Johnson aged 3, each described on the Census as 'nursechild'.[185]

Alfred enlisted before November 1914 and is named in the newspaper article as Alf Smith.[186]

We have no details of his military career but at the time of his death on 10 February 1918, aged 25, he was serving as a Sergeant in the 11th Battalion, The Rifle Brigade (The Prince Consort's Own). The 11th Battalion was a service battalion and was sent to France on 21 July 1915. It was engaged in various actions including the Battle of Guillemont in 1916 and the attacks on Steenbeek and Rue Des Vignes and the Cambrai Operations in 1917. His career seems to have been highly successful as we know that he achieved three promotions and that he was also awarded the Military Medal which

---

[184] Orchard Street is a turning off Pretoria Avenue, Walthamstow.
[185] A nursechild may have been informally adopted or fostered or be being looked after, usually for payment.
[186] Walthamstow, Leyton and Chingford Guardian 20 November 1914 p8

must have happened after March 1916.[187] Alfred was killed in action near Ypres and is buried in The Huts Cemetery, West-Vlaanderen, which is 6 Kilometres south-west of Ypres.

At the start of 1918, with Russia now out of the war, the Germans had finished fighting in the east. They were able to move many experienced troops to the Western Front and prepare for a major attack. Germany needed to win the war as quickly as possible as the effects of the British blockade of German ports meant food was now becoming scarce in Germany.

The German plan was known as the Kaiserschlacht, or Kaiser's battle, and its first phase, Operation Michael, was planned to start in March. Its objective was to break through the Allied lines and advance north-westerly to seize the Channel ports and drive the army into the sea. The British troops could hear the preparations behind the German lines as trains brought troops to the Front. In the early hours of 21 March 1918, the Germans began an enormous bombardment which lasted for about five hours and caused considerable damage to the British trench lines. Taking advantage of fog, the highly trained German troops attacked and captured 21,000 British prisoners on the opening day, as well as guns. Reinforcements were rushed to the front and on the following day, 22 March, intense fighting continued. Much of the land gained after the Somme Offensive of 1916 was lost. Fighting continued throughout the rest of March and, by early April, the Germans had advanced 40 miles into Allied territory.

On 9 April in Flanders, the Germans launched a second attack, Operation Georgette, with a massive bombardment. Following intense fighting, German gains continued over the next few days and the situation looked critical for the Allies. On 11 April,

---

[187] The Military Medal was a Level 3 Award, awarded for gallantry and devotion to duty when under fire in battle on land and instituted on 25th March 1916 for other ranks of the British Army and Empire Forces. On the reverse of the medal is inscribed "For Bravery in the Field".

Haig issued a special order of the day, which concluded
> 'With our backs to the wall and believing in the justice of our cause each one of us must fight on to the end. The safety of our homes and the Freedom of mankind alike depend upon the conduct of each one of us at this critical moment.'[188]

The Allied troops had been forced to retreat, giving up much hard won ground, to the Green Line, a recently constructed and unfinished defence trench line where they were given the order by Haig, 'This position must be held at all costs – to the last man.'[189]

Operation Georgette was stopped on 29 April after heavy fighting, particularly around the town of Villers-Bretonneux, near Amiens. By now, the German soldiers were exhausted and had out-run their supplies of manpower and food by advancing so far and so fast. The Spring Offensive had achieved some territorial gains but the advance could not be sustained nor the war won. Conditions at home were worsening with many basic resources in short supply, the Americans were in France and Germany had lost the war at sea. Estimated casualty figures for the Spring battles give French casualties in the region of 92,004 and British as 236,300, a total of about 328,000, and German casualties as 348,300.

During the course of the German Spring Offensive, two "Boys" lost their lives and a further two were to die in the follow up battles.

Edward John Rollings was born in Holloway on 19 May 1898 and died just short of his twentieth birthday. He was baptised on 14 August 1898 at St John's Church, Holloway[190] and lived with his parents, Robert, a railway clerk, and Amy at 39, Wedmore Gardens, off the Holloway Road. By April 1901, they had moved to Walthamstow and were living at 14, Nicholson Road,[191] with three older siblings. Edward joined Blackhorse Road School from the

---

[188] Draft Order for the day 11 April 1918. D. Haig.
[189] Ibid
[190] St John's Church dates from 1828 and is still open.
[191] Nicholson Road has been demolished but stood on the corner of Forest Road (south side) and Blackhorse Lane (east side).

Infants' School on 11 June 1906 and left, aged 14, on 5 June 1912. By April 1911 Edward and his parents had moved to 22, Coleridge Road, south of Forest Road. One other sibling and Arthur Johnson, a boarder, were also living in the house. The Census records that the family had had five children, one of whom was deceased. Edward enlisted in Stratford before November 1914[192] and must have lied about his age as he was only 16 years old. To enlist at that time, no proof of age was required. [193] He was in France by 1 January 1915 and served throughout the war. He was awarded the 1914-15 Star and the British and Victory Medals.

Edward achieved three promotions and was serving as a Sergeant in the 1st Battalion, The King's (Liverpool) Regiment, when he was killed in action on 16 April 1918 in the region of Boisleux-St. Marc. Boisleux-St. Marc is 8 kilometres south of Arras and was occupied by Allied troops in March 1917 following the German withdrawal but, from April to August 1918, part of the village was once again in German hands. On the same day that Edward was killed, the regiment's Private Jack Counter won the Victoria Cross for crossing open land under heavy fire with no cover to get vital information from the front line. A party of troops, followed by six other men, had previously tried and all been killed. The information he carried enabled his commanding officer to organise and launch the final successful counter-attack. We do not know if Edward was one of those men.

Edward is buried in Cabaret Rouge British Cemetery, Souchez, on the Arras to Bethune road. On 23 August 1918 payment of £21.0.9d (£21.4p) outstanding pay was paid to his mother and on 2 December 1919, she was paid his War Gratuity of £21.10.0d (£21.50p).

---

[192] Walthamstow, Leyton and Chingford Guardian 20 November 1914 p8
[193] A man wishing to enlist could do so providing he passed some physical tests and was willing to enlist for a number of years, usually seven. He had to be at least 5 feet 3 inches and aged between 18 and 38 (although he could not be sent overseas until he was aged 19). The Territorials would accept 17 year olds. From August 1914, men could enlist for three years or the duration of the war.

Archibald Thomas Smith was born on 19 March 1898 in Tufnell Park and was baptised on 8 May 1898 at St Andrew's Church, Fulham.[194] His parents Thomas, a porter, and mother, Diana, lived at 22, Humbolt Road, Fulham near the Queen's Club. Thomas and Diana Bligh Smith, a domestic servant both gave 22, Humbolt Road as their address when they married on 10 February 1897 at St Andrew's.

In April 1901 Archibald was named as Archie on the Census and the family had moved to 11, Warrender Road, Tufnell Park and he attended Burghley Road School, Tufnell Park.[195] Thomas was now working as a railway guard, and there was a younger sibling, Ernest. By December 1907 the family had moved to 29, Sterling Road, Higham Hill, Walthamstow and Archibald and his brother joined Blackhorse Road School on 2 December. In April 1911 there was a further child and Thomas was now working as a passenger guard on the Midland Railway. Archibald left school on 29 March 1912, aged 14.

We do not have Archibald's service record but he was serving as a Private in the 1st/13th (County of London) Battalion, the Princess Louise's Kensington Battalion, when he was killed in action in the Arras area on 25 April, having previously served in the 9th Battalion, The London Regiment. He has no known grave and is commemorated on the Arras Memorial.

On 5 September 1918, a payment of £6.3.6d (£6. 15.5p) outstanding pay was made to his mother with a further payment of £0.7.4d (£0.39p) on 17 September 1918. Archibald's War Gratuity of £5.0.0. was paid to his mother on 4 December 1919.

His mother, still living at 29, Stirling Road, died on 13 February 1938 and probate of her will of £341.19.8. (£341. 98p) was granted to her husband Thomas, a retired railway guard, on 2 April 1938.

---

[194] St Andrew's Church, Fulham was built in 1873 to serve the growing population of the area. It is still in use today.
[195] Burghley Road Board School opened in 1884. Now part of Acland Burghley School.

Joseph Pooley was born on 22 January 1893 in Wood Green. By 1901, the family were living at 18, Southwell Road, Croydon, and his father, Richard, was working as a plasterer. Richard and Sarah had seven children. The family must have moved to north London as, on 14 January 1904, Joseph joined Blackhorse Road School from Earlsmead School, Tottenham,[196] and the family had moved to 35, Tavistock Avenue, Walthamstow. Joseph left school on 27 July 1908, aged 15, for the Technical School. By April 1911, he was working as a junior clerk and the family were now living at 17, Fairfield Road, Higham Hill. The family had eight living children, three others were deceased. Joseph enlisted in Colchester, initially in the Essex Yeomanry. At the time of his death on 11 May 1918, he was 25 and serving as a Private in the Somme area with 9th Battalion, The Essex Regiment. He is buried in Mailly Wood Cemetery, Mailly Maillet, which lies 9 kilometres north of Albert.

On 7 December 1918 payment of £14.7.8d (£14.38p) outstanding pay was made to his mother and on 27 November 1919 his War Gratuity of £14.0.0 was paid to his father.

On the same day as Joseph was killed, Ernest Harvey also died. He died in Number 47 Casualty Clearing Station of wounds received in the fighting around Amiens. **Ernest James Harvey** was born on 25 June 1897 in the Somerstown[197] area of St Pancras. In 1901 he was living with his parents, William and Agnes, and two siblings at 47, Barclay Street,[198] St Pancras. His father was a car man and they had two lodgers. Ernest joined Blackhorse Road School from

---

[196] Earlsmead Board School opened in Broad Lane in 1897. A school still exists on the site.
[197] Somerstown is the area north of St Pancras, Kings Cross and Euston Stations. It included some of London's worst slums which were gradually cleared after 1906.
[198] Barclay Street no longer exists. It ran north from Aldenham Street.

Medburn Street School, St Pancras,[199] on 31 August 1908 after the family moved to 70, Chatham Road off Tavistock Avenue. By 1911, William was working as a railway porter and there were eight children, seven of whom were at school. Two other children had died. Ernest left school on 16 June 1911, shortly before his fourteenth birthday.

In the winter of 1915, Ernest James Harvey married Amelia Matilda Reason in Walthamstow. On 15 January 1917, they had a son, Leslie Ernest, born at home at 131, Lynmouth Road, Walthamstow and registered by his mother on 26 February 1917. Ernest is recorded as a Railway worker so he had not enlisted by then.

In 1901, Amelia Matilda Reason and her parents, William and Matilda, and her six siblings were living at 23, Cranbrook Road, Walthamstow. By 1911, she was a school girl, aged 13, and was living at 25, Coppermill Lane, Walthamstow, with her parents and two older siblings. Given the home location, it is possible she attended Blackhorse Road Girls' School at the same time as Ernest was attending the Boys' School.

We do not know when Ernest enlisted or if he was conscripted, but, at the time of his death, on 11 May, aged 21, he was serving as a Rifleman with "A" Company of the 2nd/10th Battalion, The London Regiment (City of London Rifles). He is buried in Croy-Sur-Somme British Cemetery, about 16 kilometres north-west of Amiens. The cemetery was used between April and August 1918 for burials from the 5th and 47th Casualty Clearing Station,[200] which were at the village.

There is a mystery attached to Ernest Harvey, however, which will probably never be solved. Whilst his Commonwealth War Graves Commission details link him to William and Agnes Harvey as his parents, and not to his wife, Amelia, the

---

[199] Medburn Street School, St Pancras, opened 1877. Original buildings demolished. School became Sir William Collins Secondary School, then South Camden Community College and is now Regent High School.

[200] 47 Casualty Clearing Station (CCS) was at Crouy from April 1918-August 1918.

tiny amount of his service record that remains has him born at Brightlingsea, Essex. His details, i.e. service number, 324372; regiment, London Regiment (City of London Rifles); rank; date of death and cemetery are the same on both documents. There was an Ernest John Harvey born in Brightlingsea in the summer of 1897 so his age at death was also 21, however, this Ernest's parents were Alfred and Alice. It is impossible to explain away the possible confusion but we are confident we have identified the correct Ernest. This is supported by the evidence of how his outstanding pay and War Gratuity were paid out. The register of soldier's effects has £3.19.0 (£3.95p) paid to Ernest's widow, Amelia, on 30 September 1918 with a further sum of £7.18.0d (£7.90p) paid to her on 16 November for their son, Leslie. His War Gratuity of £3.10.0d (£3.50) was paid to Amelia on 11 December 1919.

In June 1919, just a year after Ernest's death, Amelia Matilda Harvey married John W Wisker, 1892-1944, an ex-soldier who had served in the Royal Field Artillery. He was discharged on 30 October 1918 on medical grounds owing to gunshot wounds to his left leg resulting in amputation. They had two children. Amelia died in Waltham Forest in 1974. Ernest and Matilda's son, Leslie, died in 1978, aged 61.

The third Blackhorse Road teacher to die was **Flemming William Goddard** who, at 39 years and 7 months, was the oldest "Boy" to lose his life. He was born in Shoreditch on 12 October 1878 and in April 1881, aged 2, he was living at 127, Fort Road, Bermondsey, with his parents John, a tin plate worker, and Mary, two siblings and a lodger. From the 1891 Census it appears that the family moved between Hoxton (Shoreditch) where Flemming (1878) and Samuel (1885) were born and Southwark where Catherine (1877 in Walworth) and Charles (1881 in Bermondsey) were born. In April 1891, a scholar aged 12, he was living at 4, The Links, near Stoneydown Avenue, Walthamstow, and a fourth sibling had been born. By 24 August 1891 they had returned to Southwark as Flemming was admitted to Comber Road School, Southwark,[201] and the family was living at 5, Barkworth Road. They had returned to Walthamstow by April 1901 and were all living at 31, Greenleaf Road. Unhelpfully, the enumerator does not record any of the family members' occupations.

The Blackhorse Road Boys' School Log Book records that Flemming was on the staff on 1 April 1903 and that he sat his Scholarship Examination in December 1903. On 15 May 1905 he commenced duties as an Assistant Master (Certificated) and in 1906 both Flemming and his brother, Samuel, were working at Blackhorse Road Boys' School. On 11 August 1909, Flemming married Emily Bethell[202] Fox, a spinster, in Epping. Emily was born in Wimbledon in 1888 and in 1901 her family were living at 299, High Road, Loughton. In April 1911, Flemming and Emily were living at 118 Winchester Rd, Higham's Park, Chingford, and he was a Certificated Teacher at a Council School, working for Walthamstow Education Committee. They moved to Garethowen, The Avenue, Chingford and in the Autumn of 1911, their son, Dennis was born and registered in Epping.

A substantial portion of Flemming's Service Record exists so we are able to piece together much of the last three years of his life. On 13 May 1915, aged 36, Flemming attested at Walthamstow to serve for four years in the Territorials or for the duration of the war. On 17 May 1915, stated as being in the 3rd East Anglian Field Ambulance at Peterborough, he agreed to serve overseas if required.[203] He was posted to the regular army, the 2nd/3rd East Anglian Field Ambulance, in Blackpool on 30 March 1917 and was sent overseas as a replacement on 18 June 1917, embarking from Southampton for Le Havre where he arrived the following day. He travelled to Marseille where he embarked on 1 July 1917 aboard

---

[201] Comber Grove School opened in 1877. Closed or reorganised in the 1950s.
[202] Bethell – Hebrew meaning from God's house.
[203] Territorial soldiers had to agree to service overseas.

the Hospital Transport Ship *'Kingsfaun Castle'* [204] for Alexandria where he landed and joined Base Depot Mustapha on 6 July 1917. On 25 July 1917 he was attached to the 1st/3rd (Lowland) Field Ambulance unit for duty in the field. On 10 April 1918 he embarked from Alexandria on the S.S. *'Caledonia'*[205] with the 1st/2nd. (Lowland) Field Ambulance for France, disembarking at Marseilles on 17 April 1918.

On 27 May 1918 he was at St Eloi when the Germans shelled the town. At about 4.00 a.m. one of the first shells landed on a hut where Flemming and other personnel from his unit were. The regimental diary records that ten other ranks, including Flemming, were killed instantaneously, 5 other ranks died later of wounds, ten other ranks were slightly injured and 6 other ranks were seriously injured. He is buried in Ecoivres Military Cemetery, Mont-St. Eloi with eleven other RAMC men who were buried on the same day. The cemetery is 8 kilometres North West of Arras. Emily Bethell Goddard added 'Via Crucis Via Lucis' ('The way of the Cross is the Way of the Light' from the Stations of the Cross) to the standard phrasing on the headstone. The 17 letters cost 4/11. (£0.25p). He is also commemorated on the Chingford War Memorial.

Emily was living in the 'Sisters' Huts, Royal Victoria Hospital, Netley, Hampshire,[206] probably working as a volunteer nurse,[207] when she was informed that her separation allowance of 19/6 (97.5p)[208] would cease on 8 December 1918. From 9 December 1918 Emily was awarded a pension

---

[204] H.M.S. Kingsfaun Castle, Armed merchant ship and troopship.
[205] S.S. Caledonia commissioned as a troopship 29 December 1917.
[206] Netley Hospital was near Southampton. During the war a large Red Cross hutted hospital was built at the back of the hospital, which allowed a further 2,500 beds and over 50,000 patients were treated there. The hospital was demolished, apart from the chapel, in 1966.
[207] Many of the staff were Red Cross volunteers, as most of the regular staff were overseas.
[208] Separation allowances were paid to dependents when a soldier was posted away from home. In Emily Goddard's case the allowance was replaced with a widow's pension.

of 20/5d (£1.0.5d [£1.2½p]) per week for herself and one child. On 12 September 1918, probate on Flemming's estate of £462.11.01 (£462.55p) was granted to William Bethell Fox, gardener and Emily's father.

On 27 September 1918 the army wrote to Emily to forward Flemming's possessions. They were his identity disc, sundry papers, a photo case, two religious books, a book of poems, four water colour brushes, a razor strop and photos. On 1 October 1918, Emily acknowledged receipt. At that time she was living at Garethowen, The Avenue, Chingford.

When she was sent notification on 9 October 1919 of his Memorial Scroll and 'Death Penny', she was living with her parents in Loughton. She returned the form stating

> 'I am returning herewith the form sent to me for completion with regard to plaque and scroll.
>
> I have to thank you but I do not think should care to have one of these.
>
> I am able to visit the grave in France occasionally, and think a beautiful memory is all I need.
>
> I am
>
> Yours faithfully
>
> E. B. Goddard.'

On 30 December 1920, the police at Loughton responded to a request from Army Records who were trying to locate Emily. The report stated that she 'still resides at 1, Albert Villas, High Road, Loughton, Essex or can be contacted at Ivy Lodge, Acton Green, London, W4, where she is employed during the week, returning to her Loughton address at weekends.' In 1920, Flemming was listed in the National Union of Teachers

War record.

On 16 February 1922, the Loughton police were further involved when they replied to the Army that they had spoken with Emily's mother and that Emily did not want his medals. Mrs Fox agreed to ask her daughter to reply to the Army's letter about the medals when she returned to Loughton at the weekend. Despite this, on 27 February 1922, Flemming's British War and Victory Medals were dispatched.

Why did Emily reject Flemming's death plaque and his medals? From the information we have, i.e. he served in the RAMC where he would not have carried a weapon; he was carrying religious books; the religious inscription Emily added to his gravestone; the rejection of the medals, it seems likely that she and Flemming were religious. It is possible he was a conscientious objector whose views precluded killing and that he volunteered for service in 1915 as a non-combatant in the RAMC to save lives rather than take them. Some conscientious objectors refused to engage with the war in any way, others took on non-combatant work, some, like Flemming, facing very real dangers. Perhaps this is why Emily refused his medals

After Flemming died she was working in Acton, possibly using her wartime experience as a nurse. She died a widow, aged 62, in 1950. Dennis is not named in her will so perhaps he too predeceased her.

After the ending of the German advance in late April 1918, fighting continued on the Western Front. During this fighting, George Allen and Frederick Keen were killed.

George Edward Allen was born on 1 October 1898 in Bethnal Green. He was baptised on 16 July 1899 at St Andrew's Church,[209] Bethnal Green. The family were living at 279, Wilmot Street,[210] Bethnal Green. By April 1901 they had moved to 92, Gosport

---
[209] St Andrew's Church, Bethnal Green, 1831-1981.
[210] Wilmot Street was part the Waterlow Estate, made up of tenement blocks, which was built in the second half of the 19th century south of Bethnal Green Road at the Cambridge Heath Road end.

Road, by Walthamstow Cemetery, with George's parents Edward, a plasterer, and Mary and three siblings. Another couple and their child also lived in the house. The family moved to 4, Walpole Road, off Palmerston Road, and George attended the Infants' School and then joined the Boys' School on 11 June 1906. The 1911 Census records him as being 12 years old, at school, having been born in Bethnal Green to Edward and Mary Allen, the second of 10 children eight of whom were still living. They had moved again, this time to 42, Farnborough Avenue. George left school on 4 December 1912, aged 14.

We have no record of his occupation although we may speculate that he worked for the Post Office as he served in the 8th (City of London) Battalion (Post Office Rifles) London Regiment, having enlisted on 15 May 1915, when he was only 16.[211] The regiment was sent to France on 25 January 1917 and fought in various actions in France and Belgium during 1917, including the Menin Road Ridge, Polygon Wood and Second Passchendaele. In 1918 they were in the Somme region including at Villers Bretonneux. George was promoted to Corporal but was killed on 25 July and has no known grave. He was 19 years old and is commemorated on the Pozieres Memorial[212] in the Pozieres Cemetery, a few miles North East of Albert, with other members of the Post Office Rifles. George's father received payment of £16.12.1d (£16.60p) outstanding pay on 7 February 1919 and his War Gratuity of £15.10.0d. (£15.50p) on 3 December 1919.

Frederick Albert Keen was born on 28 April 1899 in Bethnal Green. In 1901 he and his father, also called Frederick, a cabinet maker, and his mother Edith, were living at 4, Salcombe Road, Stoke Newington, close to the present A10 or Great Cambridge Road. Between 1902 and 1905 the family moved to Walthamstow and were living at 22, Tavistock Avenue when Frederick joined

---

[211] The minimum enlistment age in 1915 was 18.
[212] The Pozieres Memorial commemorates over 14,000 United Kingdom and 300 South African Forces casualties who have no known grave and who died in the Somme region from 21 March to 7 August 1918.

Blackhorse Road School from the Infants' on 3 June 1907. In April 1911, Frederick was still at school and the family had moved round the corner to 58, Century Road. He now had five siblings and all six children had survived infancy. He left school on 2 May 1913, aged 14.

His Service Record states that Frederick was working as a fish porter and was living at 20, Tavistock Avenue, when he enlisted in Stratford in the 100th Training Reserve Battalion, at the age of 18 years and 2 days on 30 April 1917. He was 5 feet 4 1/2 inches tall. A curiosity from his record is that it appears Frederick and his mother had been living at 2, Albert Road, Three Counties, Arlesey, Bedfordshire and later 15, Asylum Road, Arlesey, Bedfordshire, during his training, before moving back to 20, Tavistock, Avenue, Walthamstow. On 18 December 1917, his mother was paid £0.9.2d (0.46p) a week allowance and requested having the allowance paid out at Pretoria Road, Post Office, Walthamstow rather than in Arlesey.

On 1 April 1918 Frederick was transferred to a regular battalion, The Royal Sussex Regiment, joining them on 3 April. On 7 April 1918 he was transferred to 7th Battalion, The East Kent Regiment (The Buffs) and allocated a new regimental number, G/14200, having been 46357. He joined his battalion on 8 April and was posted to 'A' Company in the field on 13 April 1918.

Frederick was killed in action serving as a Private with "D" Company, The Buffs (East Kent Regiment) on 6 August 1918, aged 19, at Authie in the Somme and is buried in Beacon Cemetery, Sailly-Laurette, which is 19 Kilometres east of Amiens and 9 Kilometres south-west of Albert. He was probably re-buried after the war from a battlefield cemetery.

On 29 October 1918 his personal effects comprising cards, cigarette case, photos and letters were sent to his mother. He was awarded the War and Victory Medal. On 8 July 1920, his mother was sent his Memorial Plaque.

On 8 August 1918 the Allies launched a series of offensives against the Germans on the Western Front, starting with the Battle of Amiens which pushed the Germans back across France, forcing them to retreat beyond the Hindenburg Line.[213] The offensives came to be known as 'The Hundred Days'.[214]

'The Hundred Days' was the most costly period of the war for "The Boys" with 13 losing their lives, 25% of the total losses. Between 9 August and 13 November, John Blackmore, William Peachey, Leslie Conway, Reginald Sellers, Jarvis Engley, Albert Smither, Robert Tresadern, Sydney Bartram, Alfred Cox, Sidney Day, Albert Mills, Cecil French, and George Mills were all to die. In addition, Louis Simmonds was to die in a Prisoner of War Camp.

Unfortunately there is scant information about many of "The Boys" killed in this phase of the war. **John Blackmore** was born in Mile End on 25 October 1899. In April 1901 he was living in Carlisle with his parents, Charles, a travelling Post Office sorter,[215] and Sarah. Two of his siblings were born whilst they lived in Carlisle but by 30 September 1907, they had moved back to London, first to Harlesden and then to 8, Blenheim Road when John joined Blackhorse Road School. The 1911 Census states that his father was a Postal Worker and that a fourth child had died. John left the school on 19 December 1913 aged 14. He enlisted in Walthamstow in 1917. We do not have his service record but know he served as

---

[213] The Hindenberg Line (or Siegfried Line) was a series of formidable, well defended German defensive areas stretching from Tilloy, south-east of Arras, in the north to near Vailly on the Aisne in the south.

[214] The 'Hundred Days' does not refer to a specific battle or to a unified strategy, but to the rapid series of Allied victories over 95 days which ended on 11 November 1918 with the signing of the Armistice. 'The Hundred Days' were amongst the most costly of the war with British casualties totalling 350,000, 200,000 of them between the start of September and 9 October, of which 140,000 were suffered at Cambrai-St. Quentin. Only the first battle of the Somme was more costly. The difference was that the Allies finally achieved all of their objectives.

[215] Travelling Post Office sorters travelled on the mail trains sorting mail en route. Mail trains operated in Britain between 1855-2004.

a rifleman in the King's Royal Rifle Corps and was posted to 12th Battalion London Regiment (The Rangers). He was killed in action on 9 August 1918, aged 18, during the Battle of Amiens and, like George Allen, is buried in Beacon Cemetery, Sailly-Laurette.

William George Peachey was born on 4 December 1899 in Holloway. On 10 June 1900 he was baptised at St John's Church, Upper Holloway,[216] by which time he and his parents, George and Martha, were living at 25, Blackhorse Road, Walthamstow. George was a bricklayer. By April 1901 they had moved to 53, Blenheim Road and Mrs Fletcher, William's maternal grandmother was living with them. Despite living so close to the school, William attended St John's School, Pemberton Gardens, Holloway[217] until, on 29 March 1909, aged 9, he joined Blackhorse Road School. By April 1911 William had five siblings aged between nine and one. He left school on 12 December 1913, aged 14.

We do not have much of William's Service Record but he was serving as a Private in the 2nd/10th Bn. London Regiment, having served in the City of London (Rifle Brigade), when he was killed in action, aged 19, on 15 August 1918 during the British advance. He is buried in Bray Vale British Cemetery, Bray-Sur-Somme which is situated 8 kilometres south-east of Albert and 16 kilometres west of Peronne. It is likely that his body would have been brought in, probably after the Armistice, from one of the battlefield cemeteries in the Somme region. On 13 January 1920 payment of £5.0.6d (£5.2 ½p), including his War Gratuity of £5.00, was paid to his mother.

Reginald Gordon B Sellers claims the distinction of being born furthest from Walthamstow. He was born on 26 November 1895 in Somerford Magna (or Great Somerford), Malmesbury, north Wiltshire. On 14 May 1900 Reginald, aged four and a half, and his

---

[216] St John's Church, Upper Holloway consecrated 1828. Designed by Charles Barry whose other work included the Houses of Parliament. Since 1978, it is known as St Peter with St John, Upper Holloway.
[217] St John's School was adjacent to the church and designed by Charles Barry. Opened in 1831. Moved to new site 1967-1972.

sister, Rebe, aged three and a half, were enrolled at Great Somerford Church of England School. Their address was given as Broad Somerford. The 1901 Census was taken on the night of 31 March and Reginald was living at 32, Chippenham Road, Great Somerford, with his parents Adolphus, a self employed builder working from home, his mother, Mary, and four younger siblings including his sister, Rebe, and brother, Leslie who was born in 1898. Both Reginald and Rebe left the school on 4 April 1901 but they must have moved to Walthamstow shortly afterwards as Reginald attended Blackhorse Road Infants' School, transferring to the Boys' School on 1 April 1903. The family were living at 57, Tavistock Avenue. He left the school on 28 October 1909, aged nearly 14. The register states that he left the district. However, he was actually old enough to leave school and the family's next address is Blenheim Road, only one road further from the school. By April 1911, now aged 15, he was working as an Insurance Clerk, the family had moved to 39, Blenheim Road and his father was now categorised as a joiner. Reginald's four siblings were still alive but two other siblings had not survived infancy.

Reginald was serving as a Private in the 4th Battalion, The City of London Regiment, Royal Fusiliers when he was killed, aged 22, on 27 August 1918. The regiment was fighting in the Battle of the Scarpe between 26-30 August, a phase of the Second Battle of Arras. He is buried in Peronne Road Cemetery at Maricourt on the Albert-Peronne Road. His body may well have been brought there from a battlefield cemetery, after the war. On 20 November 1918 outstanding pay of £1.16.8d (£1.83p) was paid to his mother. A further sum of £9.17.8d (£9.88p) was paid to his mother on 3 April 1919 and on 11 December 1919, his War Gratuity of £11.10.0d (£11.50p) was paid to her.

Reginald's brother, Leslie Adolphus Sellars, served in the Royal Navy and survived the war.

Leslie John Henry Conway was born in Stratford on 3 August 1898 and was an only child. In April 1901 he was living at 8,

Colchester Avenue, Manor Park, off the Romford Road, with his father, John, a grocer and his mother, Sophia, and her sister. He joined Blackhorse Road School on 30 September 1909 from Monega School, Upton Park, the family having moved to 52, Blenheim Road. In 1911, Leslie was still at school and his father was now an Off Licence Beer retailer. Sophia and her sister had now been joined in the house by their mother, Leslie's grandmother. Leslie left school on 6 September 1912, aged 14.

Little of Leslie's Service Record exists but we know he enlisted in Stratford in August 1916 and served in the Northumberland Fusiliers before being transferred to the 1st/5th Battalion, Alexandra, Princess of Wales's Own Yorkshire Regiment where he served as a Private. He was reported missing in action, presumed killed, in the Somme region, on 29 August 1918, aged 20. His body was recovered and he is buried in Vendresse British Cemetery, which is located 16 kilometres south of Laon. He was owed 1d wages when he was killed. On 7 June 1920, payment of £22.18.1d (£22.91p), including his War Gratuity of £11.10.0d (£11.50p), was paid to his sole legatee, his mother Sophia.

Albert Henry Smither was born on 14 July 1895 in Bethnal Green. In 1901, aged 5, he was living at 20, Crescent Place, Bethnal Green,[218] with his parents Benjamin, a band sawyer, his mother Elizabeth and three siblings. The Smithers moved to Tottenham and then to Walthamstow and Albert joined Blackhorse Road School on 7 November 1904 from Page Green School Tottenham,[219] The admissions register has the family living at 45, Kings End Road but this may be an error and actually be King Edward's Road as no Kings End Road can be found in London. Albert left school on 16 July 1909, aged 14. Two years later the family were living at 11, Hervey Park Road, Walthamstow and Albert was working as a wood boring machinist. There were now two more children but two

---

[218] Crescent Place was a cul-de-sac, now demolished, situated near the present day Columbia Road Market off Hackney Road.
[219] Page Green School Tottenham opened 1882, closed 1963 having been a secondary school from 1934.

others were deceased.

Albert's Service Record exists almost in its entirety and it provides a fascinating glimpse of the last four years of his life, a life full of both incident and adversity, not always creditable, but ending in his untimely death. Albert attested on 8 August 1914 in Walthamstow and is one of "The Boys" named in the local newspaper article.[220] Albert had a letter of support to enlist, dated 8 August 1914, from his employers, Harris Lebus, Furniture Manufacturers.[221] On his Attestation Form and in Lebus's letter of support, his address is noted as 32, Farmer Avenue, Walthamstow however, also in his service record, his mother is noted as his next of kin living at 32, Farnborough Avenue. We can find no record of a Farmer Avenue in Walthamstow and it is possible the address on the Attestation Form was copied from Lebus's letter. Farnborough Avenue is a short distance from the school, off Forest Road. Albert's occupation is given as a Wood Machinist although the letter states that he was an apprentice. He was initially allocated to the 7th Battalion, The Essex Regiment. On 9 September 1914, Albert signed that he was willing to serve overseas. He must have initially impressed as, on 4 November 1914 he was promoted to Lance Corporal.

On 24 July 1915, the regiment embarked for the Middle East from Devonport on board H.M.T. *Southland*,[222] and on 22 August

---

[220] Walthamstow, Leyton and Chingford Guardian 20 November 1914 p8
[221] Harris Lebus was England's largest furniture manufacturer in the early 20th Century, employing over 1,000 people. The family originated from Germany opening their first London factory in 1857. Their factory was in Tottenham Hale (later the GLC depot) where it is likely Albert worked. During the War they produced munitions including ammunition boxes and stretchers. The firm lost a large number of employees to the forces and many never returned. Regular parcels of comforts were sent to the volunteers. Prior to the firm being taken over in 1981, they produced chipboard furniture at a factory on Blackhorse Lane.
[222] H.M.T. Southland launched July 1900 as SS Vaderland. Requisitioned as a troopship and renamed H.M.T. Southland, she was operating in the Aegean carrying men to Gallipoli. On 2 September 1915, she was torpedoed with 37 fatalities. She was repaired but was again torpedoed in April 1917 off the Irish coast and sank with the loss of four lives.

he was admitted to hospital in Suvla Bay with bronchial problems and catarrh. He was discharged back to his unit on 28 August. On 29 November 1915 he was admitted to hospital in Malta with tonsillitis. On 4 February 1916 he rejoined his unit at El Daaba in Egypt and on 15 February 1916 he was admitted to hospital in Alexandria as 'Sick no wound'. On 1 April 1916 he embarked from Alexandria for England. From 10 April 1916 to 8 May 1916, he was posted to the Military Convalescent Hospital, Woodcote Park, Epsom with Valvular Disease of the Heart (V D H.)[223] On 8 May he was in the County of London War Hospital, Epsom with Disordered Action of the Heart (D A H)[224] and was then posted to Command Depot. On 26 May he was posted to the Eastern Command. From 27 May he was in the Eastern Command Depot, Shoreham-By-Sea with suspected pleurisy and D A H. His medical reports indicate a possibility of rheumatic fever as a child. He spent 29 days in hospital and did some light work and leg drill. Somewhat surprisingly, on 20 June 1916 he was marked as A1 fit. However, on 21 October he was marked as B1 and on 1 September at Catterick, he was classified as C1. Despite this, on 12 December 1916, he was posted to the 2nd/4th Royal Scots.

In early 1917, Albert, aged 21, married Dora Fisher, aged 20, in Norwich.

On 5 November 1917 he was serving at Edinburgh Castle when he committed an offence deemed to be 'Conduct to the prejudice of good order and military discipline.' and was reprimanded on 7 November. On 26 March 1918 while stationed at Portobello he was 'Absent without leave having been wired to return to unit from

---
[223] V D H or Valvular Disease of the Heart possibly a physical abnormality of the heart - perhaps due to something like rheumatic fever in childhood.
[224] D A H or Disordered Action of the Heart known as 'Soldier's Heart' or 'Effort Syndrome' and thought to result from a combination of over exertion, mental stress and fatigue. 2,503 out of 33,919, or 7.4 per cent, of the soldiers and sailors invalided from the services from the beginning of the war up to May 31st 1916, were discharged on account of heart disease.

tattoo 9.30 pm till 11.30 p.m.' and on 28 March he was punished by being deprived of his Lance Corporal's stripe and forfeiting two days pay.

On 1 April 1918 he wrote his will leaving everything to his wife and on 2 April 1918 embarked for France, arriving on 3 April 1918. On 17 July 1918, he was guilty of a further offence, this time being in the field and having a dirty rifle on parade. He was punished with seven days confined to barracks.

On 12 September 1918 his regiment was in the field as part of 37th Division, one of three divisions of the Third Army which attacked the village of Havrincourt which was defended by four German divisions. The other Divisions were the 62nd (West Riding) Division and a New Zealand Division. The 62nd took Havrincourt and the 37th took nearby Trescourt.

During the day, Albert was reported missing in action. His body was never recovered and he is commemorated on the Loos Memorial.[225] He was 23 years old.

On 20 February 1919 Dora, as Albert's sole legatee, was awarded his outstanding pay of £1.3.2d. (£1.16p) and on 3 December 1919, his War Gratuity of £22.16.10 (£22.84p).

On 20 February 1919, the War Office sent Albert's personal effects to Dora at 9, Branford Road, Sprowston Road, Norwich. They consisted of postcards, photos, cigarette case, letters, pocket case, visiting cards and comb. The War Office stated that any medals due to Albert were to be sent to Dora. She would also have received his scroll and Death Penny. They were sent from Army HQ Hamilton to her on 7 April 1919 and signed for by her in Norwich on 14 May 1919. On 10 April 1919 Dora

---

[225] The Loos Memorial forms the sides and back of 'Dud Corner' Cemetery at Loos-en-Gohelle on the Loos Battlefield. It stands on the site of a German strong point, the Lens Road Redoubt, captured by the 15th (Scottish) Division on the first day of the battle in 1915. (See James Vickery). The name comes from the large number of unexploded shells found in the area. The Memorial commemorates over 20,000 officers and men who have no known grave, who died in the area, many in 1918.

was awarded a weekly War Widows Pension of either £0.13s 9d (68p) or £0.18s.9d (93p) (It is impossible to decipher the copy). On 8 May 1921 Dora Smither acknowledged receipt of Albert's 1914-15 Bronze Star for his service as Lance Corporal. He was also awarded the Victory and British Medals. It is fair to speculate, given his medical record, whether Albert should have been made to continue in active service and to what extent his disciplinary issues related to his poor health. We will never know.

In 1925, Dora re-married in Norwich to William Francis. She died in 1974.

Albert's brother Benjamin (Ben) also enlisted and is named in the newspaper article.[226] He survived the war and lived to be 90, dying in 1986.

Jarvis J Engley was born in Southwark on 22 August 1897. In 1901 he was living at 13, Bush Road, Bermondsey, near Greenland Dock, with his parents, Jarvis, a porter butcher, and Ellen and two siblings. He was baptised at Saint Barnabas' Church, Rotherhithe,[227] on 28 May 1902. By 17 April 1905 the family had moved to 27, Bunyan Road, Walthamstow, when Jarvis joined Blackhorse Road School. The Admission Register does not record his previous school. In 1911 he was a scholar living with his parents and two siblings. His father was now a butcher salesman but his sister Iva had died in 1908 aged 8. He left school on 1 September 1911, aged 14. By 1918, his family had moved to 39, Russell Road, Forest Road.

We have little of Jarvis's Service Record however we know he served in the Grenadier Guards[228] in 1916. His service number is 24831 which indicates he joined the regiment in December of 1915.[229] We cannot establish whether he enlisted in the Guards or

---

[226] Walthamstow, Leyton and Chingford Guardian 20 November 1914 p8
[227] Saint Barnabas' Church, Rotherhithe built 1870-1872; demolished in the 1960s.
[228] The Grenadier Guards is the most senior regiment of the Guards Division of the British Army and can trace its history back to 1656.
[229] The Grenadier Guards has all of their enlistment records from 1881. The enlistment numbers for each year fall within a particular range so soldiers with numbers from 24627-25068 joined in December 1915.

was transferred from another regiment to infill.

On 27 September 1918 the Allies launched an attack along the Canal du Nord as part of the drive to push back the German army. Because of the success of the attack, the road to Cambrai was open to the allies. The 1st Battalion, The Grenadier Guards, played a key role in the battle and Captain (Brevet Major, Acting Lieutenant-Colonel) Gort[230] was awarded the Victoria Cross. Jarvis was killed in action. He was 21 years old and is buried in 'Sanders Keep' cemetery at Graincourt-Les-Havrincourt. The battle cost 30,000 allied casualties and an unknown number of German casualties. 36,500 Germans were taken prisoner.

On 20 June 1919 Jarvis's outstanding pay of £17.5.9d (£15.29p) was paid to his mother and sole legatee, Ellen, as was a further sum of £3.14.6d (£3.72 ½p) on 30 June. His War Gratuity of £13.10.0d (£13.50) was paid to her on 2 December 1919).

On 6 March 1920 he was awarded the Victory Medal and the British War Medal.

On 27 September, the same day and in the same battle as Jarvis lost his life, **Robert Richard Tresadern** was also killed. He was serving as a rifleman in the 16th Battalion, London (County of London) Regiment (Queen's Westminster Rifles).

Robert was born on 1 February 1898 in Walthamstow. In 1901 his family was living at 69, Ritchings Avenue, just south of Forest Road, with his parents George, a compositor, and Elizabeth and five siblings. He joined the school on 11 June 1906 from the Infants' School. By then, the family had moved further south to 11, Ringwood Road, off Markhouse Road.

According to the School Log Book, in November 1909, he won a scholarship to the School of Art and in July 1910 he won a scholarship to a Higher Elementary School. He left Blackhorse Road School on 2 September 1910 to take up his scholarship. He

---

[230] Field Marshal John Standish Surtees Prendergast Vereker, 6th Viscount Gort, VC, GCB, CBE, DSO and two Bars, MVO, MC (1886–1946). Commanded the British Expeditionary Force sent to France in 1939 which was evacuated from Dunkirk.

was noted as at school on the April 1911 Census so presumably he did go on to the Higher Elementary School. The family had now moved the short distance to 46, Somerset Road, off Queens Road and eight children are named on the Census although it confusingly reports seven living and one deceased. On 17 June 1913, aged 15, Robert was registered as a Temporary Boy Clerk in the Civil Service.[231] The war was to end his career with the Civil Service and he enlisted at Westminster.

We have some details of his service record and know he was serving from 18 March 1917. Assuming he was serving in 16th Battalion, London (County of London) Regiment (Queen's Westminster Rifles) he could well have seen significant action as the regiment was part of 56th Division which took part in a continuous series of battles. The First Battle of the Scarpe from 9–14 April, the Third Battle of the Scarpe from 3-4 May, both part of the Battles of Arras, the Battle of Langemarck from 16-17 August, a phase of the Third Battle of Ypres, the capture of Tadpole Copse on 21 November, the capture of Bourlon Wood from 23-28 November and fighting German counter attacks in the Cambrai area from 30 November-2 December. In 1918 the Division fought at the First Battle of Arras on 28 March, the Battle of Albert on 23 August and the Battle of the Scarpe from 26-30 August before the attack on the Canal du Nord. He is unlikely to have been involved in all of these but it does illustrate the high level of activity over this period.

On 27 September 1918, the village of Sauchy-Cauchy was captured by the 56th (London) Division. Robert was killed and is buried in Sauchy-Cauchy Communal Cemetery Extension a small cemetery with only 51 graves, 3 kilometres north of the main Arras to Cambrai road.

On 8 April 1919, a sum of £9.0.4d. (£9.2p) outstanding pay was paid to Robert's father, George, and, on 9 December 1919, he was paid Robert's War Gratuity of £10.10.0d. (£10.50p).

---

[231] The London Gazette 4 July 1913

On 6 November 1920, he was awarded the Victory and British Medals for his service from 18 March 1917 until his death on 27 September 1918.

On 30 September, two more "Boys" were to die.

Sydney John Bartram was born in Walthamstow on 26 December 1893. In 1901 he was living at 31, Melbourne Road, Walthamstow, just to the south of Forest Road, with his parents Henry, a general labourer and Mary and six siblings. It was the family's fifth different address since 1884. Sydney joined Blackhorse Road School from Markhouse Road School[232] on 27 August 1901. He left the school between 23 June 1904 and 9 January 1905 for hospital and finally left, shortly before his fourteenth birthday, on 29 November 1907.

In 1911, aged 17, he was working as a shop assistant in a fancy goods shop and living at 24, Herbert Road, Walthamstow with his parents and four siblings. There had been a total of 12 children, eleven of whom were still alive.

His immediate next movements are unknown but in the spring of 1914 he married Alma Marshal in Bridgend, Wales, and he enlisted in Maesteg in the 6th Battalion (Glamorgan) Welsh Regiment. He was to be one of the most successful "Boys" winning a Military Medal and achieving significant promotions. Unfortunately, little of his service record remains but the regiment embarked for France on the 29 October 1914, landing at Le Havre, and took up a role working in the Lines of Communication. On the 5 July 1915 they joined 84th Brigade, 28th Division and on the 23 October transferred to 3rd Brigade, 1st Division. On the 15 May 1916 the 1/6th became a Pioneer Battalion to 1st Division and saw action in the Battle of the Somme.

In 1916 Sydney was awarded the Military Medal for bravery in the field and the conferment of the medal was announced in the

---

[232] Markhouse Road Board School opened 1891, became a Secondary school from 1946 and closed 1996. Now demolished although the school railings remain.

London Gazette.[233] As the regiment fought at several of the battles in the Somme during this period it is probable that was when he won the medal.

In 1917 the regiment saw action in the German retreat to the Hindenburg Line and the Third Battle of Ypres. In 1918 they fought at the Battles of the Lys, the Second Battles of Arras, and the Battles of the Hindenburg Line from 12 September 1918.

Sydney achieved several promotions becoming a Colour Sergeant[234] and, by September 1918, he was a Company Quarter-Master Sergeant.[235] On 27 June 1918, he visited the school whilst home on leave.[236]

The Regimental Diary reports that
> 'From the 24-28 September the Battalion was employed by night upon the important work of erecting belts of wire in front of the captured positions under orders of the respective Brigades. The task was somewhat hazardous but happily was accomplished with very few casualties.'[237]

There was a further successful push the following day as part of the Battle of the Saint Quentin Canal. At some point during these days, Sydney was seriously wounded and he died of his wounds in the 12th General Hospital, Rouen, on 30 September 1918. He was 24 years old and is buried in the Saint Sever Cemetery Extension, Rouen. He had served through four years of war.

By 1918, his parents, Henry and Mary Bartram, were living at 14, Garden Terrace, Maesteg, Bridgend, Glamorgan, and his wife, Alma Ethel Bartram, was living at 197, Countess Road, Walthamstow. They were noted as his next of kin. Payment of

[233] London Gazette 14 September 1916 p 8998
[234] Colour sergeant is a non-commissioned officer ranking above sergeant.
[235] The Company Quartermaster Sergeant is the second most senior non-commissioned officer in the company. He is in charge of supplies and serves as deputy to the Company Sergeant Major.
[236] School Log Book 27 June 1918
[237] Regimental Diary

£41.6.9d (£41.34p), which included his War Gratuity of £29.0.0d, was made to his widow and sole legatee, Alma, on 5 May 1919. He was awarded the 1914 Star, the Victory Medal and the British War Medal 1919.

Alfred Aaron Cox was born in New Cross on 17 March 1893. His parents were Frederick, a coachman, and Harriet, and they lived at 60, James Street.[238] Alfred was baptised at All Saint's Church, Lambeth,[239] on 13 July 1894. On 13 January 1896, aged 2, he was admitted to his local school, Saint John and All Saints[240] in Lambeth. The family had moved to 50, Lancelot Road, a little further south of Waterloo Station so the family would have been familiar with the Victoria Palace Theatre[241] and the Canterbury Music Hall,[242] which stood nearby. By 1901 they had moved again, this time north of the Thames to 7, Babmaes Mews,[243] off Saint James' Square, Westminster. Frederick was working as a stable groom foreman and Alfred had five siblings. By 31 August 1903 they had moved again, possibly twice, to 11, Lancaster Road, off Blackhorse Lane, Walthamstow, and Alfred joined Blackhorse Road School from Wood Street School[244] which was situated in Shernhall Street, some distance from Lancaster Road. Alfred left Blackhorse Road School on 2 June 1906, aged 13, and the record states that he left the district. However, in 1911, aged 18, he was living at 97, St Andrew's Road,

---

[238] James Street has been demolished but was behind Lower Marsh Street under the taxicab approach to Waterloo Station.
[239] All Saints Church was demolished in 1901 for the expansion of Waterloo Station.
[240] Saint John and All Saints School near St John's Church, Waterloo Road. Closed 1964. Building now used as offices.
[241] The Victoria Palace Theatre in The Cut, now known as The Old Vic.
[242] The Canterbury Music Hall (1852-1942) was London's first Music Hall and stood in Westminster Bridge Road.
[243] Babmaes Mews, now Babmaes Street, would have provided stabling for the large houses in the St James' area.
[244] Wood Street School was a School Board School in Shernhall Street which closed in 1906.

a few street south, with his father, now described as a general labourer with Walthamstow Urban District Council, his mother and eight siblings. One further child was deceased. Alfred was working as a general labourer at Wright & Sons, Printers, Blackhorse Lane.

Alfred enlisted early in the war and is one of those mentioned in the newspaper article.[245] We do not have his service record but we know he was serving in the 81st Siege Battery,[246] Royal Garrison Artillery as a Gunner when he was killed on 30 September 1918, probably at the battle of Cambrai-St. Quentin, also known as the battle for the Hindenburg Line. He had survived for four years and was 25 years old. He is buried in Cagnicourt British Cemetery which is located 8 kilometres south-east of Arras on the main Arras-Cambrai road. His body was probably brought there after the Armistice. The 81st Battery had first gone to France in February 1915 and served in many of the campaigns during the war. Siege Batteries were not always attached to a Division as they were positioned according to the needs of the battles so pinpointing their actual location is difficult.

Sidney Clement Day was born in Bermondsey on 13 September 1894. In 1901 the family were living at 31, Donald Road, Plaistow. Sidney's father William was a foreman at a refreshment room and his mother, Louisa, had had two other children. By 29 April 1904, the family had moved to 28, Cassiobury Road off Coppermill Lane and Sidney joined Blackhorse Road School from Upton Park.[247] The school does not have a record of him leaving but it would have been about March or April 1908 when he was 14. In 1911, aged 16,

---
[245] Walthamstow, Leyton and Chingford Guardian 20 November 1914 p.8
[246] Siege Batteries were equipped with heavy howitzers capable of sending explosive shells in a high trajectory on to the enemy. Often used to attack enemy artillery their armaments were 6, 8 and 9.2 inch howitzers, although some had railway- or road-mounted 12 inch howitzers. Siege Batteries were not always attached to a Division as they were positioned according to need.
[247] Upton Park. This may have been Upton Cross School or Upton Lane School or it may have been their location. There was not an Upton Park School.

he was working as a fish fryer and he had moved west to 54, Forest Road, Edmonton with his parents and four siblings. His father was now working as a restaurant cook.

Sidney enlisted in Kennington and was serving as a Lance-Corporal in the 2/24 County of London Regiment (The Queens) when he was killed on 11 October 1918, aged 24, near Arras. He is buried in Bully-Grenay Communal Cemetery, British Extension, approximately 20 kilometres north of Arras.

The 2/24th (County of London) Battalion (The Queen's) served in France, Salonika, Egypt and the Western Front during the war. With very little of Sidney's record available it is impossible to know what action he saw or which regiments he served in but he did achieve promotion to the rank of paid Lance-Corporal. On 18 July 1919, payment of £21.10.0d (£21.50p) including his £15.10.0d (£15.50p) War Gratuity was paid to his father. His parents had moved again, this time to 2, The Crescent, off St James' Street, Walthamstow.

Cecil Charles French was born in Walthamstow on 19 November 1899. In 1901 he was living at 159, Forest Road with his parents Arthur George, a grocer and provisions merchant, his mother Edie (Edith) two siblings and a servant. He joined Blackhorse Road School on 11 June 1906 from the Infants' School and was still attending at the time of the Census in 1911. Cecil's father was now described as a grocer and retail dealer and there were four siblings although one does not appear on either the 1901 or 1911 Census. Cecil left school on 25 April 1913, aged thirteen and a half, for the Technical School.

We have very little of Cecil's Service Record but he enlisted in January 1917 and served as a Gunner in the 1st/16th Battalion, the London Regiment (Queen's Westminster Rifles). He was killed in action on 4 November 1918, aged 18, during the crossing of the River Aunelle as part of the final push. He is buried in Seburg Communal Cemetery which is situated about 10 kilometres east of Valenciennes and contains 19 Commonwealth burials, all from 4 and 5 November 1918.

The Allied advance had been successful and the Germans had been driven back across France and Belgium. By the end of September the German Supreme Army Command recognised that a Germany victory was impossible and advised the Kaiser to seek a ceasefire. By 5 October the Kaiser had agreed and the German government sent a message to President Wilson[248] of the United States offering to negotiate terms based on his "Fourteen Points".[249] Before there could be any negotiations, Wilson demanded that the Germans retreat from all occupied territories, cease submarine activities and the Kaiser must abdicate. Initially the German Supreme Command objected to the conditions but there was no willingness amongst the German soldiers to continue the war. Desertions were increasing and conditions at home were awful. On 5 November, the Allies agreed to begin negotiating a truce. Meanwhile, a mutiny by German sailors at Wilhelmshaven[250] began to spread across the country and on 9 November 1918, the Kaiser abdicated and a republic was declared and proclaimed.

The armistice between the Allies and Germany agreed to a ceasefire to take effect at 11 a.m. Paris time on 11 November 1918. It was not a formal surrender although, in effect, it was seen as a victory for the Allies and a defeat for Germany. The German troops were withdrawn from France and Belgium and Allied troops occupied the German Rhineland area and France occupied Alsace-Lorraine. The Armistice was signed in a railway carriage at Compiegne, near Paris and, although it ended the actual fighting, it took six months of negotiations at the Paris Peace Conference to conclude the peace treaty, the Treaty of Versailles, which was signed on 28 June 1919. Treaties were also signed with other combatants.

---

[248] Woodrow Wilson, 1856-1924, 28th President of the United States.
[249] President Woodrow Wilson's Fourteen Points was a blueprint for world peace presented on 8 January 1918. The European Allied leaders were not convinced it was workable.
[250] Wilhelmshaven – German naval base on the North Sea.

Blackhorse Road Boys' School acknowledged the Armistice.
'Armistice declared today at 11 a.m. the school celebrated the great event in a bright and fitting manner. The Committee closed the school during the afternoon session.'[251]

The final British soldier believed to have been killed in action was Private George Edwin Ellison of the 5th Royal Irish Lancers who was shot at 9.30 a.m. on the outskirts of the Belgian town of Mons, close to where the first soldier had died in 1914. Other soldiers were to die up to and beyond 11.00 a.m. on 11 November, the time and date agreed by the respective forces for hostilities to cease. Some died as hostilities continued beyond 11 November because it took time for news of the Armistice to reach them. Others, like two of "The Boys", died as a result of wounds received during the war.

One day after the Armistice was signed, **Louis John Simmonds**,[252] serving as a Private in the 2nd Battalion, Sherwood Foresters (Notts and Derby) Regiment, died of pneumonia in Friedrichsfeld Hospital, Germany. His death was registered on 26 November 1918 and he was initially buried in the British Section of Friedrichsfeld Cemetery. His body was later moved to the CWGC Cemetery within the Südfriedhof Koln, Cologne Southern Cemetery, along with British bodies from 183 cemeteries throughout Germany.[253] Louis had been reported missing on 24 April 1918, probably near Baileul, and was captured by the Germans. From his Service Record, we now know he was a Prisoner Of War[254] from 16 April until his death.

---

[251] Blackhorse Road Boys' School Log Book 11 November 1918
[252] Sometimes noted on his Service Record as Lewis.
[253] In 1922 the graves of Commonwealth servicemen who had died all over Germany were brought together in four cemeteries at Kassel, Berlin, Hamburg and Cologne.
[254] According to the School Log Book of 14 July 1916, at least three other old "Boys" were Prisoners of War, Holling, Richards and Hoskins. 'The boys sent 3 parcels of food parcels' to them.

Louis was born on 29 October 1898 in Islington and was baptised on 10 August 1900, at St Saviour's Church, Hoxton.[255] His father, John Robert, was a painter's labourer, and, with his mother Elizabeth, they lived at 12, Lampeter Street, Islington.[256] By the following year they had moved to 30, Lampeter Street, with John described as an unskilled labourer. There were two siblings, the oldest, Elizabeth aged 8, having been born in Hamilton, Ontario, Canada, and Clarence aged 10 months. In 1911, Louis was described as aged 12 and at school and they were living at 30, Shakespeare Road, Stoke Newington.[257] There were three further children. On this Census, Louis was also described as being born in Canada but this is an error by the enumerator. It does appear that John and Elizabeth emigrated to Canada between 1888 and 1898 and returned to England before Louis was born. On 8 January 1912, aged 13 years and two months, Louis joined Blackhorse Road Boys' School from Hackney. The family had moved to 16, Clifton Avenue, opposite the school. Only nine months later, he left school on 6 September, shortly before his fourteenth birthday.

Much of Louis's Service Record exists. He was working as a fitter's apprentice when he attested in Walthamstow on 11 December 1915. The following day he was allocated to the reserves. He was mobilised on 17 May 1917 when he was 18 years and nine months old in the 3rd London Regiment as Private 254083 and was posted to the 3rd Reserve Battalion on 18 May 1917. He embarked from Southampton on 24 October 1917 and landed the following day at Le Havre. On 28 October 1917 he was transferred to the Sherwood Foresters (Notts and Derby) Regiment as Private 72858 and posted to 2nd Battalion.

---

[255] St Saviour's Church, Hoxton, was severely damaged in an air raid in 1940 and was was not rebuilt.
[256] Lampeter Street has now been demolished. It was on the Hoxton/Islington border.
[257] The area, known as Albert Town, was severely damaged during the Second World War and some roads were later demolished. Probably now Shakespeare Walk.

In March 1918 he suffered several bouts of ill health necessitating visits to the Field Hospital. On 2 February he contracted tonsillitis followed on 26 February by diphtheria. Louis was returned to his unit but was reported missing on 16 April 1918. The 2nd Battalion were engaged in fighting in the defence of Baileul near the Franco-Belgian border. This was a battle fought as part of the German Spring Offensive, the Battle of the Lys, which saw the Germans take the town and the Allies have to withdraw. Louis was captured by the Germans and became a Prisoner of War in Germany. He contracted pneumonia and his death certificate, dated 28 November, states that he died in the Friedrichsfeld P.O.W. Hospital on 12 November.

At the end of the war there were many unaccounted soldiers so next of kin may have had to wait several months to establish what had happened to their relative. In Louis' case, the War Office confirmed that they had received notification of his death on 11 April 1919 and that his relatives could be informed of his death and the whereabouts of his body. His family would have been informed in April 1918 that he was missing but had to wait nearly a year for notification of his demise.

On 20 August 1918, authorisation was given that his father should receive Louis' outstanding pay of £33.15.10d (£33.89p) including his War Gratuity of £8.0.1d, his death having been officially accepted. On 25 August 1919 his father received his possessions. Louis was awarded the British War and Victory medals which his mother received and signed for on 6 February 1922.

We have chosen to group the last "Boy" to die in the War with his brother who had been killed a fortnight earlier. In less than a fortnight between 31 October and 12 November 1918, George and Mary Mills of 10, Blenheim Road lost both of their two sons. Albert, the eldest by 15 months, was killed in action, aged 20, on 31 October 1918. George was invalided home and died in hospital on 13 November, two days after the Armistice had been signed. He was 19.

Albert Edward Mills was born on 2 March 1898 in Kentish

Town and was baptised on 31 July 1898 at St John the Baptist Church, Kentish Town.[258] His parents were George Augustus, a Midland Railway Guard, and Mary, and they were living at 127, Torriano Avenue, off the Camden Road, St Pancras. His brother, **George Ernest Mills**, was born on 27 August 1899 and he was baptised on 14 January 1900 at St John the Baptist Church. By 1901 the family were living a few roads further north at 15, Countess Road and George was now described as a railway hand. The brothers attended the local Burghley Road School[259] until they left and joined Blackhorse Road School together on 30 September 1907. The family had moved to 10, Blenheim Road, Walthamstow. Albert left school on 2 September 1909, aged 12, having won a Scholarship to a Higher Elementary School.[260] George senior was absent on the night of the 1911 Census but he signed the form. On 6 September 1912, aged 14, George also gained a place at a Higher Elementary School having achieved a Higher Elementary School Scholarship

We do not have any Service Records for either brother so our knowledge of their wartime service is limited. Albert served as a Gunner in the 119th Heavy Battery, Royal Garrison Artillery. The Battery had served in France since 1914. Albert died on 31 October 1918 and is buried in Grevilliers British Cemetery which is located 3 kilometres west of Bapaume.[261] It is highly likely that Albert was brought to the Casualty Clearing Station and died there. The battery would have been supporting Allied attacks as the Germans were

---

[258] Now the Christ Apostolic Church, Highgate Road.
[259] Now Ackland Burghley School.
[260] School Log Book, 9 September 1910
[261] Grevillers was occupied by the Allies on 14 March 1917 and in April and May, the 3rd, 29th and 3rd Australian Casualty Clearing Stations were located nearby. The cemetery was used until March 1918, when the German took Grevillers. On 24 August, the New Zealanders recaptured Grevillers and in September, the 34th, 49th and 56th CCSs were set up in the village and the cemetery used again.
After the Armistice, over 250 graves were brought in from outlying battlefields cemeteries.

driven back.

George was a Private in the 1st/5th Battalion, West Yorkshire Regiment (Prince of Wales's Own) having previously served in the 97th Battalion, Training Reserve. We may assume that he was wounded in the 100 Days advance and was returned to England where he died in the 5th Southern Hospital, Portsmouth,[262] on 13 November 1918. Their parents inserted an article in the local paper.[263]

They also had inscribed, at a cost of £0.18.8d (£0.94p), a tribute to Albert on George's gravestone in Queen's Road Cemetery. 'Also in memory of Gunner A.E. Mills who died in France October 31st 1918, aged 20 years.'[264] (See Illustrations section.)

KILLED IN ACTION.

MILLS.—Mr. and Mrs. Mills, of Blenheim Road, Walthamstow, wish to convey to the many kind friends and neighbours their sincere thanks for the kind expressions of sympathy shown to them on the loss of their two dear sons, Albert Edward, who died in France, October 31st, aged 20, and George Ernest, who died in the 5th Southern Hospital, Portsmouth, on November 13th, aged 19 years. Also for the beautiful floral tributes and other marks of respect shown by them on the occasion of the funeral of the latter on November 19th, and to assure them that it was a source of great comfort to them in their great sorrow.

And so the war ended and the surviving participants went home. Final casualty figures are not accurate but there were approximately 700,000 British casualties or about 11.5% of the

[262] The 5th Southern General Hospital covered hospitals in the Portsmouth and Gosport area which were under military control.
[263] Walthamstow, Leyton and Chingford Guardian 28 November 1918
[264] Imperial War Graves Commission Report.

6 million personnel mobilised. 12% of ordinary soldiers were killed compared to 17% of officers including over 50 Generals. Of the "Blackhorse Road Boys", of the 1,000 or so who attended between 1901 and 1910, assuming three-quarters enlisted, the percentage is slightly lower at about 7.5%.

The war necessitated a steep learning curve as armies adapted to new demands of warfare. The British Army had dispensed with its red tunics before the Boer War but protection for troops was slow to develop. Steel helmets were not available until early 1916 and there was no body protection for the effects of shrapnel. Using heavy shelling bombardments to 'soften' up the enemy required huge quantities of munitions and it took until 1916 for industry to adapt to the demands. Even then, there was a disproportionate number of dud shells. Developing long range firing to allow bombardments of targets which were out of sight made attacking safer and this, coupled with the creeping barrage technique meant troops could advance behind the shelling with less risk of being hit by their own side. The nature of trench warfare meant that Generals had to review and revise their strategy and it took until 1918 for this to become fully effective. Other technological developments included flame throwers, the use of gas and tanks. On the Home Front, there was a need to develop a strategy to balance the increased demands for personnel to staff the army whilst not depleting the home industries which led to denoting some jobs as reserved occupations. It also saw the increase in women working in factories and other jobs.

Across the country, there was a need for families to adjust to the fact that, although many of their loved ones were returning, some, such as "The Boys", would not be coming home.[265] Some who returned could be considered 'the lucky ones' with the chance to fulfil their lives, perhaps going on to father children who attended Blackhorse Road. However for many, across the country, there was

---
[265] British and Empire casualties in 1918, dead, wounded, missing and prisoner, totalled 3,190,235, from a total force of 8,904,467, (35.8%) of whom 908, 371 (10.2%) were confirmed dead.

a struggle to find work, there was the need to adjust to family life, sometimes with wives and children they had seen little of for several years. Some women, having enjoyed the independence of working, had to give up their jobs whilst, for single women, there was the realisation that they may not find a husband. There were also huge numbers who survived, but at the cost of their physical or mental health, and who lived out their lives with permanent reminders of the war. Perhaps surprisingly, it was not until 1928 that one the major effects of the war reached its peak. In that year, 10% of all men claiming disability pensions were diagnosed with shell shock.

Chapter 6

The reports of my death have been greatly exaggerated[266]

Eric Cottew, Stanley Robarts, James Staines

In the previous five chapters we have recorded the lives and deaths of 52 of the names on the War Memorial. There are, however, three other "Boys" who we believe were named in error and who survived the war.

Eric Guy Campbell Cottew was born in Islington on 17 September 1896. According to the 1901 Census, Eric, aged 4, was living with his father, Arthur, a Stockbroker's Clerk, and his mother, Edie, at 12, Fulbrook Road, Islington. He joined Blackhorse Road Boys' School on 11 April 1904 from the Infants' School. His name was first written down in the roll as Cobben and then crossed out so it was probably a mis-spelling. The family was living at 9, Wellington Road, off Forest Road. According to the School Roll, Eric left the school on 2 September 1910 for London although by then he was old enough to leave school. By the 1911 Census, Eric was 14 and living at 63, Church Hill, Walthamstow, with his father, now described as an Investor in stocks and shares, and his mother and four siblings. The move indicates that Eric's father was successful in his business.

We can find no further record of Eric's education but in September 1914 he enlisted in the Warwickshire Royal Horse Artillery.[267] He was commissioned as a Second Lieutenant,[268] the only "Boy" to hold officer rank, and joined his regiment in France on 30/31 January 1915. The event was reported by Edward Manifold who witnessed his arrival.

---
[266] Mark Twain 1835-1910
[267] The Warwickshire Royal Horse Artillery was a Territorial Force formed in 1908. It was the first Territorial Force artillery unit to go to France in 1914 and spent the war on the Western Front.
[268] London Gazette 20 October, 1914

'Hoyland departs on leave on the Saturday night and life goes on as usual on these two days, except that Siggers is rather off-colour with dysentery. A new officer from the Terriers[269] is attached to us on the 3th. His name is Cottew – a full lieutenant.'[270]

We have no details of Eric's service over the next 20 months. The regiment took part in the Second Battle of Ypres fighting at the Battles of Frezenberg from 9–13 May, and Bellewaarde Ridge on 24 May. In 1916, the division was in reserve at the Battle of Flers-Courcelette on 15 September. For reasons unknown, Eric relinquished his commission on 28 September 1916. Although the British army structure traditionally reflected society, this changed during the war as 'rankers' gained battlefield promotions, but to go the other way was highly unusual. However Richard Holmes states that 'I know of at least two examples of the process in reverse.'[271] In both cases the soldier resigned owing to ill-health and, once recovered, could not regain their commission and serve abroad. Both men re-enlisted as privates and both were killed. Whether this is what happened to Eric we do not know but it is a possibility as he did not withdraw from the war. On 28 November 1916, he re-enlisted at Woolwich as a Gunner in the Royal Horse and Field Artillery. He was 6 foot 6 1/2 inches tall, much taller than other "Boys" where we have their records, and was living at 22, Clarendon Road, Leytonstone. He was described as the head of the household, aged 20 years 60 days, and of independent means. He was posted overseas on 4 May 1917.

Eric served in the army after the end of the war but not without incident. From 4-10 July 1919 he was reported overdue from leave from 'E' battery, RHA. He rejoined on 21 July 1919 and was deprived of 10 days pay and forfeited 6 days pay for overstaying his leave. He was in trouble again on 7 September 1919 when he was caught drinking in a cafe during prohibited hours and given 14

---
[269] Terriers - Territorials
[270] Diary of Edward Walford Manifold 30/31 January 1915.
[271] Richard Holmes. The Western Front. (BBC Books 1999) p 12

days Field Punishment. Returning to England, on 2 October 1919 at Bramshott, he was stated to have a disability. He was discharged from the army on 15 October 1919. He received his 1915, Victory and General Service Medals. Eric died, aged 76 in 1972. On official records, his name was sometimes mis-written as Cotton.

There are several outstanding questions about Eric Cottew. How did he get a commission? We do not know what happened to him between when he left Blackhorse Road and enlisting but, at the beginning of the war, his background of Blackhorse Road Boys' School would not normally have been seen as appropriate for officer training. Grammar and Public schools were considered a more appropriate background. It is possible his father's professional success was a factor. As to why he gave up his commission, as the lowest ranking commissioned officer he would have had serious responsibilities and the casualty rate for Second Lieutenants was disproportionately high. Illness or injury are also possibilities, however, the regiment saw little action in the months leading up to September 1916. So was there another reason for him going? Perhaps he was under pressure for reasons to do with how he performed his duties or for his behaviour, although we have no evidence to support this. He chose to re-enlist as a 'ranker', presumably as noted above, because he could not get another commission. Alternatively, perhaps he recognised responsibility was not for him.

As to why his name is on the War Memorial, was his leaving the service in September 1916 misinterpreted as his demise and his re-enlistment and survival not spotted? Having survived the war, how did he spend the rest of his life and did he ever have contact with any of his ex-schoolmates who also survived?

The last two of "The Boys" survived the war, however, both had brothers who did die but did not attend Blackhorse Road Boys' School. It is perhaps because of that that the confusion occurred that resulted in their names being recorded on the memorial.

Stanley Radnor Robarts was born in Walthamstow on 25 May 1894. In 1891, Henry Martyn Robarts, a bookseller's assistant, and

Clara and their two children, Henry and Emily, and Henry's mother, Ester, a dressmaker, were living at 5, Claremont Villas, Higham Hill Road, Walthamstow. The name was mis-written as Roberts. By 1901 they were living at 123, Higham Hill Road. Henry Martyn was now a publisher's agent. The family name was again mis-written as Roberts.

Stanley joined Blackhorse Road Boys' School on 2 June 1902 from Blackhorse Infants' School. In 1904, Henry Robarts died aged 40, leaving £424.4s.0d (£424.20p) to Clara. Stanley left school on 31 July 1908 aged 14 years. The 1911 Census records him as, aged 16, an assistant in a booksellers and living at 3, Tavistock Avenue, Walthamstow, with his mother, Clara aged 46, a widow, and his siblings Henry and Emily. One other child was noted as deceased.

We do not know anything about Stanley's war service, however we do have details of his older brother's service. Henry Martyn Robarts was born in Peckham in 1886. He was an Assistant Librarian with the Walthamstow Public Libraries Service when he enlisted in August 1914. He rose to the rank of Sergeant-Major in the Royal Army Medical Corps before applying for a commission. He was a 2nd Lieutenant in the 4th Battalion, The Norfolk Regiment, when he was badly wounded on 22 September 1917 whilst under fire. He died of his wounds on 26 September in the 8th Casualty Clearing Station.[272] Henry is buried in Duisans British Cemetery, Etrun, about 9 kilometres west of Arras

Henry had married Edith Amy Butcher in 1911 and they lived at 8, Cairo Road, Walthamstow. After Henry's death, Edith did not re-marry and died, aged 73, on 6 July 1957 in Clacton.

The local paper report refers to Henry as being
> 'one of two sons, both of whom had served their country. The one is dead, the other is permanently injured, and our sympathy goes out to the widowed mother as well as to

---

[272] The 8th Casualty Clearing Station was located at Etrun from February 1917.

the young widow of the deceased officer'.[273]

From this we can conclude that at some point before September 1917, Stanley had been seriously wounded but not killed. There is a record of a Stanley Radnor Robarts marrying Johan Grant, aged 25, in Ontario, Canada, on 11 December 1915. We cannot prove it is the same person but the name is quite distinctive and it is possible to speculate that Stanley, having received a permanent injury, was discharged and moved to Canada.

James Staines was born in Tottenham on 8 June 1892. The 1901 Census records him as aged 7 and living at 59, Blackhorse Lane, Walthamstow, with his parents John, a railway labourer, and Alice and four siblings, the oldest of whom was John who was 14. James joined Blackhorse Road Boys' School on 27 August 1910 from Pretoria Road School[274] and left on 25 May 1906, shortly before his fourteenth birthday. By April 1911 the family had moved to 221, Blackhorse Lane, and John senior was now a platelayer. There had been seven children, one of whom was deceased. John junior was no longer living at home as he had joined the Army in 1905. James enlisted early in the War and is noted in the newspaper article.[275] We have no other details of his war service and there is no record of his death.

John was already 14 when the school opened in 1901, having been born in Tottenham in 1887 so was beyond the school leaving age. We do not know about John's education but he had been working as a car man when he joined the army in Stratford on 19 July 1905 as a career soldier. He was serving in the 1st Battalion, The Cameronians (Scottish Rifles), when he was killed. Assuming he had been with them before the War, he would have served in India and South Africa. The regiment was in Glasgow in August 1914 and was despatched to France on 13 August, as part of the BEF, travelling from Southampton to Le Havre overnight on 14/15 August. They fought at the Battle of the Aisne between

---

[273] Walthamstow, Leyton and Chingford Guardian. 6 October 1917 p4
[274] Pretoria Road Board School opened in 1888 and closed in 1938.
[275] Walthamstow, Leyton and Chingford Guardian 20 November 1914 p8

7-10 September before being sent north to Flanders and the Ypres Salient. John was a Sergeant when he was killed in action in the Ypres area on 21 October 1914, aged 27. He has no known grave and is commemorated on the Ploegstreet Memorial. On 28 January 1915, his outstanding pay of £21.9.2d. (£21.46p) was paid to his father with a further sum of £0.16.4d. (0.83p) on 4 June. On 13 May 1919, his father received his War Gratuity of £8.0.0d.

The War Memorial inscription states J. Staines and we have concluded that, although John did not attend Blackhorse Road School, it is his name that is remembered on the memorial. Someone confused the two brothers and believed that James, the ex-pupil, had been killed.

Chapter 7

Conclusion

Despite extensive research there remain many unanswered questions about "The Boys of Blackhorse Road".

We know about "The Boys" who were killed and about some of those who were taken prisoner but what of those who joined up and were not killed? How many other "Boys" who fought in the War had their lives damaged or shortened that we do not know about? We cannot imagine the effect on the families who suffered losses, in several cases losing more than one son. Four families lost two "Boys" and, in the case of George and Mary Mills, both their sons died within a fortnight. Four other families lost another son, in addition to "The Boy", the Standcumbes losing two sons on the same day, 9 October 1917 at Arras.

For those that were left behind, there was a need to get on with their lives. We know that Ernest Harvey's widow, Amelia, and Albert Smither's widow, Dora, remarried, and that Percy Spreadborough's girlfriend, Charlotte, married someone else. However, what happened to Emily Bethel Goddard, the apparently determined and independent widow of Flemming Goddard? It does not appear that she remarried but did she go to France to visit her husband's memorial as she wrote to the War Office?

Memorials were erected across the country and 11 November became the focus of the nations' collective remembrance. Of the 52 "Boys" who died, 33 are buried or commemorated in France, 8 in Belgium, 4 in England, 2 in Malta and one each in Germany, Italy, Iraq, Palestine and Turkey.

There was much battlefield tourism in the years after the war but it is doubtful any of "The Boys" families would have been able to afford the cost of visiting the graves or monuments in France and Belgium? There would have been no possibility of visiting graves and memorials further afield.

We do not know who planned the Blackhorse Road Memorial or how they compiled the names so we do not know why they included three people we now believe did not die. Conversely, it is possible that there were there other casualties they missed. We do not know who unveiled the memorial or if was there a ceremony but we do know from the Girls' School Log Book that pupils subscribed to the memorial. It is a mystery as to why there is no record of subscriptions to the memorial or to it being set in place in the Boys' School Log Book when it is mentioned in the Girls' School Log Book.

What we can never know is what "The Boys" might have become had there not been a World War. The issue of what might have been is perhaps best illustrated in the case of Fred Mace who died in 1917. By an accident of birth his brother George who was five years younger, went on to become a solicitor, a Mayor of Waltham Forest and a Freeman of Walthamstow. Analysis of the occupations "The Boys" were in prior to enlistment does indicate that many were in more aspirational jobs than their fathers, perhaps as a result of their Blackhorse Road School education.

The experiences of "The Boys" replicate that of many working class boys across the country. There are well documented accounts of the experiences of public school boys who served in the war, many of whom joined from school. There are accounts of older men such as the "Pals" and "Chums" battalions but they tended to work together and to enlist together. Our story is unusual, possibly unique, as it represents the experiences of 55 elementary school boys and teachers who were already in employment when they enlisted, served in different regiments and fought in different theatres of war and, in many cases, would not even have known each other. What they had in common is that they all attended the same local elementary school in Walthamstow at some time between 1901 and 1911 and they failed to survive the war.

Of those where we have details, we know that "The Boys" had different experiences. Some, such as Sydney Bartram, survived almost the entire war seeing action in several battles and theatres of war, whilst others hardly saw action before losing their lives. A few achieved promotion and a few were even awarded gallantry medals, whilst some had less distinguished records. Some were volunteers, some were conscripted and some were regular soldiers. However all of them were asked to do a job that at times involved indescribable horror and no amount of film, words or re-enactment can possibly communicate what they experienced. All faced situations well beyond their experience or imagination.

Above the names of "The Boys" on the memorial is the Blackhorse Road Boys' School motto, a single word: *"Steady"*. These boys were not expected to change the world, they were not expected to do extraordinary things or see extraordinary sights. They did not expect it themselves. Their task was to know their place in society and to keep the old ways of life going as their fathers had done. When war came, however, these ordinary "Boys" from an elementary school in North East London far exceeded these expectations and, in giving their lives, helped create the world we live in today. The motto of the present Willowfield Humanities College is a quotation from Wordsworth: *"Give all thou canst."* The students of the present school can be proud to have predecessors who could not have given more.

Acknowledgements

A work such as this cannot happen without the support, knowledge and encouragement of many other people.

John Hemingway, the current Headteacher of Willowfield Humanities College, provided the impetus to carry out the research which led to this book. He commissioned the drama, "Blackhorse Boys", based on the first draft, performed by current students not much younger than "The Boys" which was a focal point of the new building's official opening and brought the audience to its feet. It also fulfilled one of his ambitions; to find out about the names on the memorial.

Councillor Chris Robbins, Leader of Waltham Forest Council, was sufficiently impressed by seeing the performance of "Blackhorse Boys" and its story about Walthamstow, that the Council provided the financial support to ensure the book's publication.

Staff at Vestry House Museum, Walthamstow, where the school's Log Books and Admission Registers and copies of the local paper are housed, provided research facilities.

Staff at Queen's Road Cemetery, Walthamstow, guided us to the graves of the four "Boys" buried there.

Staff at The Highlanders' Museum, Fort George, provided background information and photographs about James Vickery. This provided an unexpected further connection as one of their volunteer researchers had spent time in the early 1970s working as a Careers Officer in London and had given advice and guidance at another local school, Walthamstow School for Girls.

The Western Front Association provided invaluable advice and guidance on getting the book printed.

Proofing and critiquing was carried out by Dr Katherine Doolin of the University of Birmingham, a further link as the University was used as a hospital during the Great War and Ernest Nottage was treated there in 1916.

John White and Lisa Thundercliffe at Adverset Media Solutions provided helpful guidance on design and printing.

Jonathan Vernon of the Western Front Association read the final draft and provided helpful advice and wise suggestions to improve the finished version.

Eve Wilson, Headteacher of Willowfield from 1996 to 2011, suggested the research should be carried out some time ago and, she and John Hemingway, always intended that the memorial would be moved to the new school as part of the school's history and legacy. She has helped with the research as well as providing critical support and advice for improving the text, and has provided continued encouragement.

My sincere thanks go to all of the above. Ultimately, the work is mine and any errors or omissions are my responsibility.

Suggested Reading

A work of this length cannot hope to cover every aspect of the Great War. Some suggestions for further reading could include

The Battlefield Cemeteries

Before Endeavour Fades   Rose Coombes

Then and now photographs of the Western Front

The Somme Then And Now   John Giles
The Western Front Then And Now   John Giles

A general history of the Western Front

The Western Front   Richard Holmes

Life of a soldier

Tommy   Richard Holmes

The Battle of the Somme

Bloody Victory: The Sacrifice on the Somme and the Making of the Twentieth Century   William Philpott
The Somme: A New History   Gary Sheffield

General history and the 100 days

Forgotten Victory   Gary Sheffield

Women in the Great War

Women in the First World War   Neil R. Storey and
                                            Molly Housego

Gallipoli

Gallipoli Then And Now   Steve Newman

The Western Front Association
The local branch meets monthly with a wide range of high quality speakers. Contact Neil Pearce on pearce.neil@ntlworld.com for further details.

Picture Credits
1913 map – Walthamstow West; Old Ordnance Survey Maps; The Godfrey Edition
H.M.S. Mantis - NAVAL-HISTORY.NET
Willowfield School photograph –Willowfield Humanities College
All others - author's own collection including photographs from The Daily Mail postcard series issued between 6 September 1916 and 2 April 1917, reproduced from official photographs. The 105 different postcards were in various forms, black and white, colour, silver print and photogravure.

Bibliography

Badsey, Stephen	*The British Army in Battle and its Image 1914-1918* (London: Continuum UK, 2009)
Brown, Malcolm	*The Imperial War Museum Book of 1918 Year of Victory* (London: Pan 1999 [1998])
Bolton, Paul	*Education: Historical statistics Standard Note: SN/SG/4252*, 27 November 2012. House of Commons Library
Beckett, Ian	*Home Front 1914-1918* (London: The National Archives 2006
Brownlow, Kevin	*The War, the West and the Wilderness* (London: Secker and Warburg, 1979)
Castle, Ian	*London 1914-1917 The Zeppelin Menace* (Osprey. 2008)
Castle, Ian	*London 1917-1918 The Bomber Blitz* (Osprey. 2010)
Cecil Hampshire. A	*Armed with Stings* (New English Library.

Collier, Lindsay	April 1976) *Walthamstow Through Time* (Amberley Publishing. 2014)
Coombes, Rose	*Before Endeavour Fades* (Old Harlow: After the Battle, 2006 [1976])
Culbert, D	*The Imperial War Museum: World War I film catalogue and 'The Battle of the Somme'* (video). (London, Historical Journal of Film, Radio and Television, Volume 15, No. 4,1995)
Doyle, Peter.	*Great War Tommy. The British Soldier 1914-1918* (Odcombe Press Ltd. November 2013)
Holmes, Richard	*The Western Front* (London: BBC Worldwide Limited, 1999)
Holmes, Richard	*Tommy* (London: Harper Collins, 2004)
Hyde, Andrew	*The First Blitz* (Pen and Sword 2012[2002])
Lebus, L.S.	*A History of Harris Lebus 1840-1947* Unpublished manuscript 1965 at http://www.harrislebus.com/images/history.pdf
Middlebrook, Martin	*Your Country Needs You* (Barnsley, Leo Cooper; Pen and Sword, 2000)
Newman, Steve	*Gallipoli then and Now* (London: After the Battle 2000)
Powell.W.R. Ed	*A History of the County of Essex,Volume 6.* (London 1973)
Romig, Keith and Lawrence, Peter	*Walthamstow. Images of England.* (London: Tempus 1996 [2000]
Sheffield, Gary	*Forgotten Victory* (London: Headline 2001)
Smith, Steve.	*And They Loved Not Their Lives Unto Death* (Menin House. 2012)
Tomkin, Gregory	*Showtime in Walthamstow* (Walthamstow Antiquarian Society, 1983 [1967])

The Walthamstow, Leyton and Chingford Guardian– various
Blackhorse Road Boys' School Log Books

Blackhorse Road Girls' School Log Books
Walthamstow School Board Minutes, 27 February 1899
Old Ordnance Survey Maps Walthamstow West 1913.
The Godfrey Edition
Old Ordnance Survey Maps Walthamstow West 1894.
The Godfrey Edition
The Walthamstow Memorial Web Site
The Commonwealth War Graves Commission
www.ancestry.co.uk
www.forces-war-records.co.uk
www.findmypast.co.uk
Hackney Downs School Roll of Honour
at http://www.cloveclub.com/wp-content/uploads/WW1ROHa.pdf
http://www.thisismoney.co.uk/